MIDLAND RAILWAY SYSTEM MAPS

(THE DISTANCE DIAGRAMS)

Volume 4
BIRMINGHAM TO BRISTOL AND BRANCHES
SOUTH WALES
SOMERSET AND DORSET JOINT LINE

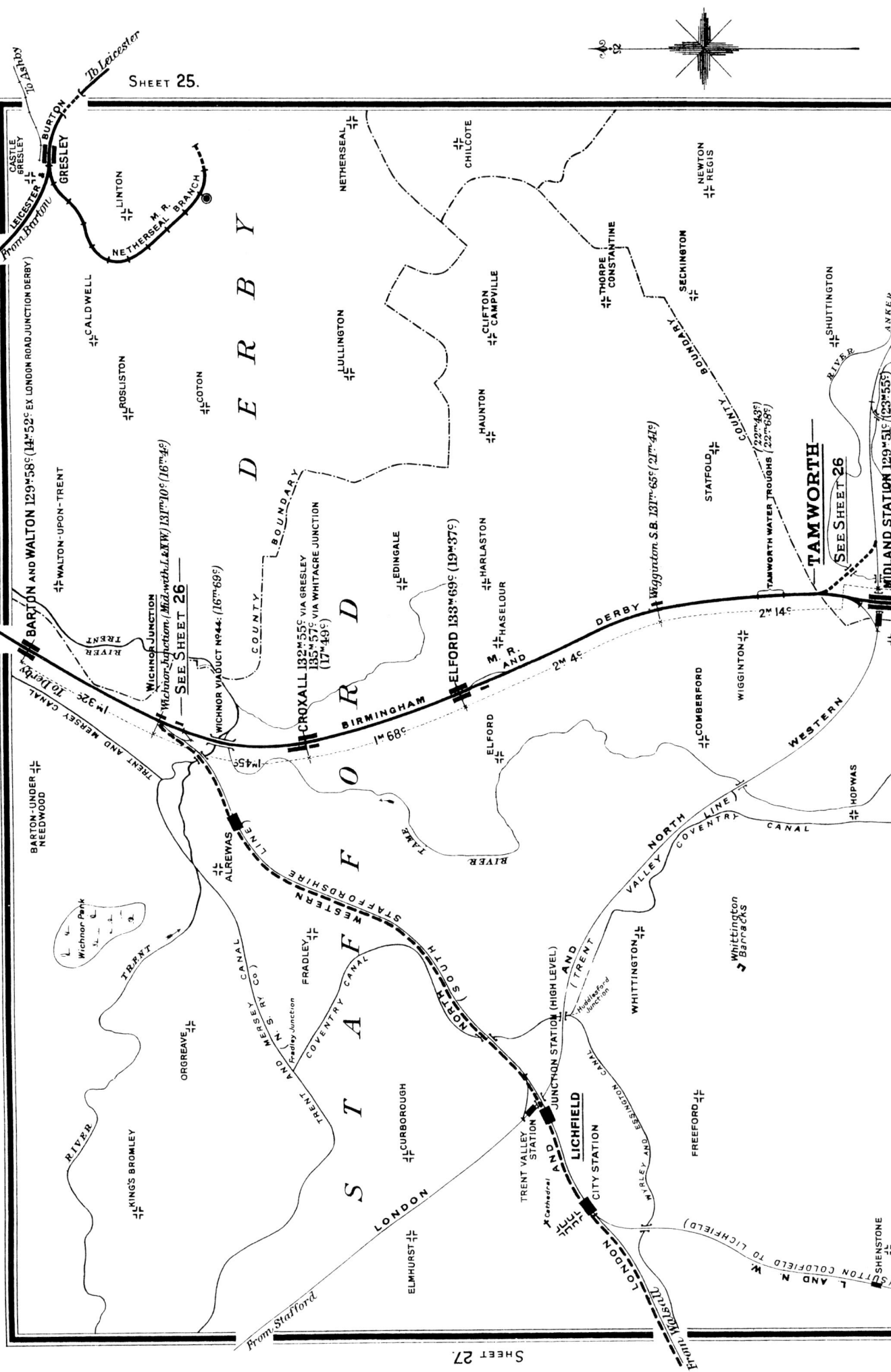

SHEET 25.

SHEET 26A.
(Seventh Edition.)

SHEET 26.

SHEET 26.

BOOK No. 76

MIDLAND RAILWAY DISTANCE DIAGRAM. SCALE 1 INCH TO 1 MILE.
TAMWORTH—WATER ORTON DISTRICT.

To Leicester

To Ashby

From Barton

CASTLE GRESLEY

BURTON

GRESLEY

LEICESTER

LINTON

NETHERSEAL BRANCH

NETHERSEAL M.R.

CALDWELL

ROSLISTON

COTON

WALTON-UPON-TRENT

RIVER TRENT

BARTON AND WALTON 129 M 58 C (14 M 52 C EX LONDON ROAD JUNCTION DERBY)

Wichnor Junction (Mid. with L. & N.W.) 131 M 10 C (16 M 48 C)

Wichnor Junction

WICHNOR VIADUCT No 44. (16 M 69 C)

SEE SHEET 26

1 M 32 C To Derby

TRENT AND MERSEY CANAL

BARTON-UNDER-NEEDWOOD

Wichnor Park

RIVER TRENT

KING'S BROMLEY

ORGREAVE

DERBY

NETHERSEAL

CHILCOTE

NEWTON REGIS

ULLINGTON

CLIFTON CAMPVILLE

THORPE CONSTANTINE

SECKINGTON

COUNTY BOUNDARY

HAUNTON

EDINGALE

HARLASTON

HASELOUR

CROXALL 132 M 55 C VIA GRESLEY
135 M 57 C VIA WHITACRE JUNCTION
(17 M 49 C)

ELFORD 133 M 69 C (19 M 37 C)

BIRMINGHAM

ELFORD

1 M 68 C

1 M 45 C

1 M 89 M

M. R. AND DERBY

STATFOLD

COUNTY BOUNDARY

SHUTTINGTON

RIVER ANKER

Wigginton S.B. 131 M 65 C (21 M 4 C)

7 (22 M 43 C)
(22 M 68 C)

TAMWORTH WATER TROUGHS

WIGGINTON

COMBERFORD

2 M 4 C

2 M 14 C

TAMWORTH
SEE SHEET 26

MIDLAND STATION 129 M 51 C (23 M 55 C)

S T A F F O R D

RIVER TAME

WESTERN

NORTH

STAFFORDSHIRE LINE

NORTH AND SOUTH

FRADLEY

Fradley Junction

COVENTRY CANAL

TRENT AND MERSEY CANAL

N.S. RY Co.

ALREWAS

CURBOROUGH

ELMHURST

From Stafford

LONDON

TRENT VALLEY STATION

Cathedral

JUNCTION STATION (HIGH LEVEL)

LICHFIELD

CITY STATION

WYRLEY AND ESSINGTON CANAL

From Walsall

LONDON

WHITTINGTON

Whittington Barracks

Huddlesford Junction

FREEFORD

AND TRENT VALLEY

NORTH VALLEY (COVENTRY LINE)

WESTERN

HOPWAS

COVENTRY CANAL

CANAL

SHENSTONE

L. AND N.W. (SUTTON COLDFIELD TO LICHFIELD)

SHEET 27.

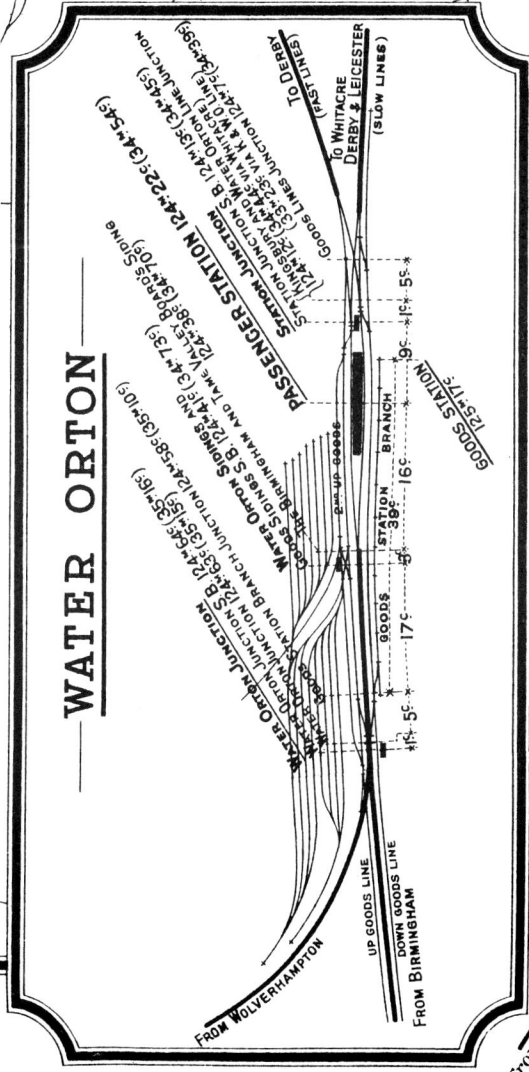

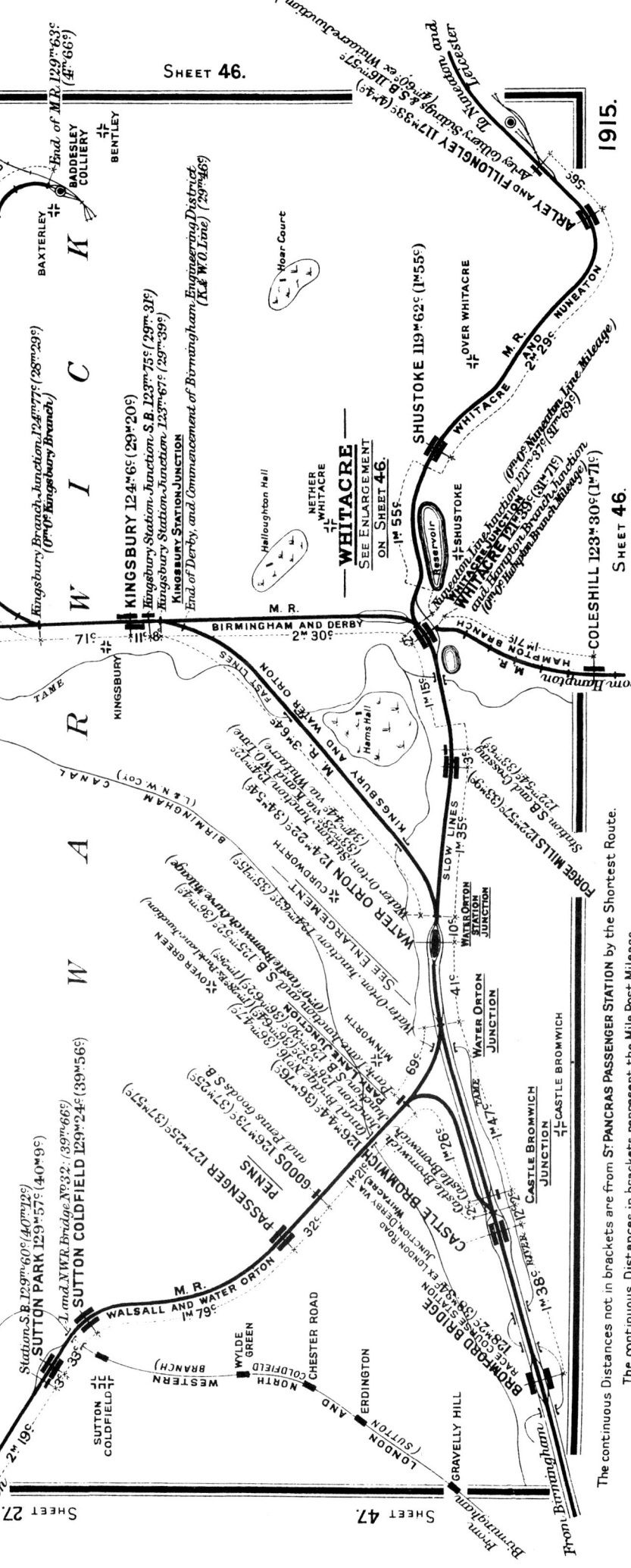

1915.

WATER ORTON

The continuous Distances not in brackets are from St Pancras Passenger Station by the Shortest Route.

The continuous Distances in brackets represent the Mile Post Mileage.

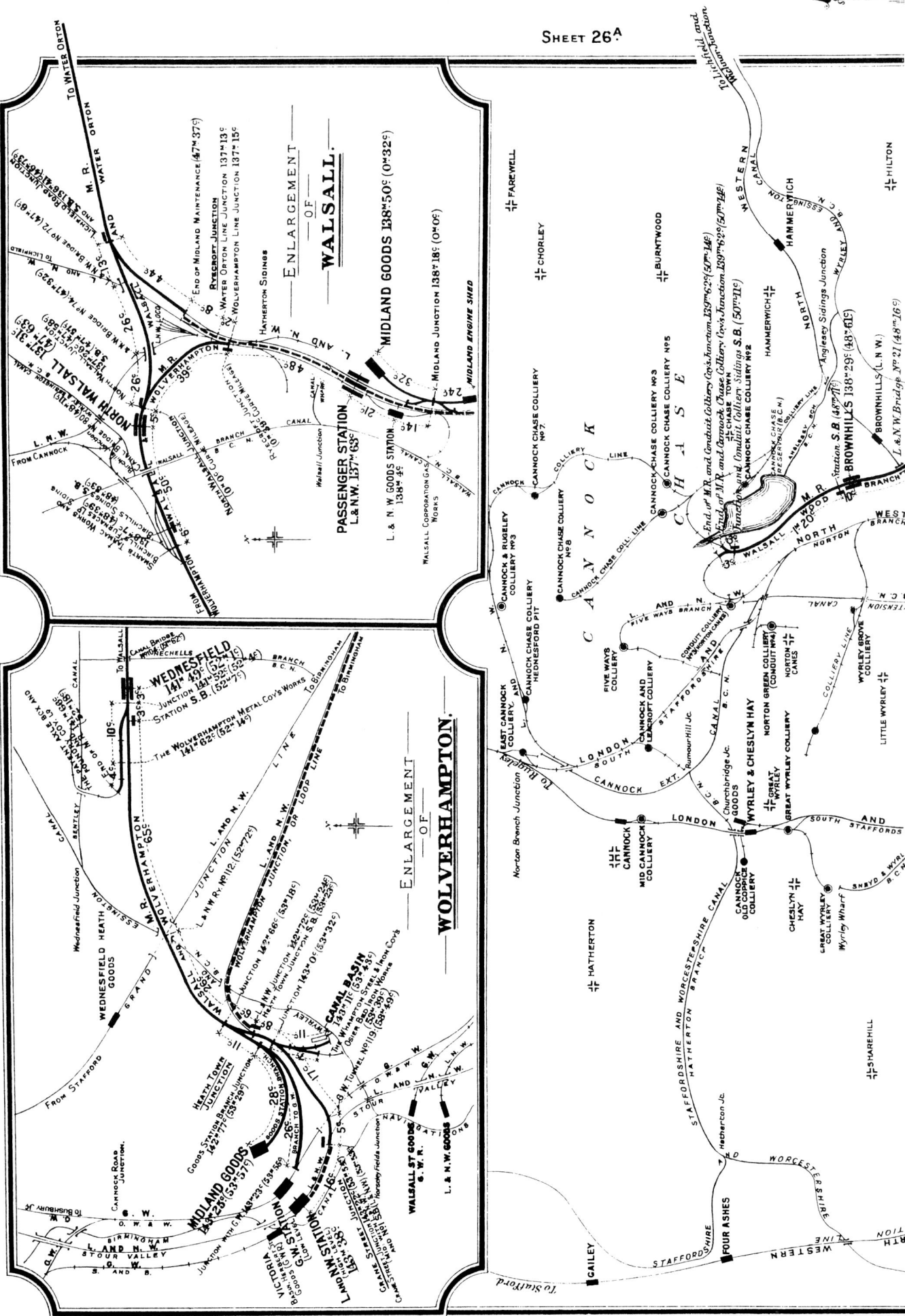

SHEET 27.
(Eighth Edition.)

MIDLAND RAILWAY DISTANCE DIAGRAM. SCALE 1 INCH TO 1 MILE.
WOLVERHAMPTON DISTRICT.

BOOK Nº 76

— ENLARGEMENT — OF — WALSALL.

TO WATER ORTON

End of Midland Maintenance (47ᴹ 37ᶜ)
Ryecroft Junction
Water Orton Line Junction 137ᴹ 13ᶜ
Wolverhampton Line Junction 137ᴹ 15ᶜ
Hatherton Sidings

MIDLAND GOODS 138ᴹ 50ᶜ (0ᴹ 32ᶜ)
Midland Junction 138ᴹ 18ᶜ (0ᴹ 0ᶜ)
MIDLAND ENGINE SHED

NORTH WALSALL

PASSENGER STATION L.& N.W. 137ᴹ 63ᶜ
L.& N.W GOODS STATION 138ᴹ 4ᶜ
Walsall Junction
Walsall Corporation Gas Works

L. AND N.W.

FROM CANNOCK

FAREWELL
CHORLEY
BURNTWOOD
HAMMERWICH
HILTON

WESTERN CANAL

CANNOCK CHASE COLLIERY Nº7
CANNOCK CHASE COLLIERY Nº3
CANNOCK CHASE COLLIERY Nº5
CHASE TOWN
CANNOCK CHASE RESERVOIR (B.C.N.)
CANNOCK CHASE COLLIERY Nº2

C A N N O C K   C H A S E

Anglesey Sidings Junction
HAMMERWICH
NORTH
WALSALL WOOD
BROWNHILLS 138ᴹ 29ᶜ (48ᴹ 6ᶜ)
BROWNHILLS (L.N.W.)
L.& N.W Bridge Nº21 (48ᴹ 16ᶜ)
Station S.B. (48ᴹ 7ᶜ)
WEST BRANCH
B.C.N.

CANNOCK CHASE COLLIERY Nº8
CANNOCK & RUGELEY COLLIERY Nº3
Cannock Chase Colliery Hednesford Pit
FIVE WAYS BRANCH
FIVE WAYS COLLIERY
CONDUIT COLLIERY
CANNOCK AND LEACROFT COLLIERY
NORTON GREEN COLLIERY
NORTON CANES
WYRLEY GROVE COLLIERY
LITTLE WYRLEY

EAST CANNOCK COLLIERY
To Rugeley
Norton Branch Junction
Churchbridge Jc.
Rumour Hill Jc.
CANNOCK EXT.
WYRLEY & CHESLYN HAY
GREAT WYRLEY COLLIERY
SOUTH STAFFORDS
SNEYD & WYRLEY B.C.N.

LONDON
CANNOCK
MID CANNOCK COLLIERY
CANNOCK OLD COPPICE COLLIERY
CHESLYN HAY
GREAT WYRLEY COLLIERY
Wyrley Wharf

HATHERTON

STAFFORDSHIRE AND WORCESTERSHIRE CANAL
Hatherton Jc.
FOUR ASHES
STAFFORDSHIRE
GAILEY
To Stafford

SHARE HILL

WEST WORCESTER LINE

— ENLARGEMENT — OF — WOLVERHAMPTON.

TO WALSALL
Canal Bridge Wednechells
WEDNESFIELD 141ᴹ 49ᶜ (52ᴹ 4ᶜ)
Junction S.B. (52ᴹ 7ᶜ)
Station 141ᴹ 52ᶜ (52ᴹ 4ᶜ)
BRANCH B.C.N.
The Wolverhampton Metal Coy's Works 141ᴹ 62ᶜ (52ᴹ 14ᶜ)
To Birmingham
To Birmingham

WEDNESFIELD GOODS
Wednesfield Junction
WEDNESFIELD HEATH GOODS
FROM STAFFORD
CANAL

HEATH TOWN JUNCTION

L. AND N.W. LINE
WALSALL JUNCTION
WOLVERHAMPTON
L. AND N.W. JUNCTION
WOLVERHAMPTON JUNCTION 142ᴹ 66ᶜ (53ᴹ 18ᶜ)
L.A N.W.R. Nº112 (52ᴹ 72ᶜ)
WOLVERHAMPTON S.B. (53ᴹ 32ᶜ)
Junction 143ᴹ 1ᶜ (53ᴹ 23ᶜ)

CANAL BASIN
The Wolverhampton Steel & Iron Coy's
Osier Bed Iron Works
MIDLAND GOODS
HEATH TOWN JUNCTION

STOUR VALLEY NAVIGATIONS

Cannock Road Junction
To Bushbury Jc.
VICTORIA BASIN GOODS G.W. STATION
L.AND N.W STATION
Goods Station Branch Junction
BRANCH TO G.W.R.

BIRMINGHAM STOUR VALLEY
WALSALL ST GOODS G.W.R.
L. & N.W. GOODS

G.W.
G.W. AND A.W.

To Stafford

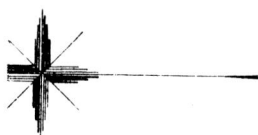

1920.

W A R W I C K

COUNTY OF STAFFORD

S T A F F O R D

To Water Orton and Birmingham

STREETLY 131^{m}75^c (43^{m}31^c) (42^{m}29^c)

County Boundary

SUTTON PARK 129^{m}57^c (40^{m}9^c)

2^{m}22^c

LITTLE ASTON

2^{m}39^c

Aldridge Junction 134^{m}38^c (44^{m}70^c)

WATER ORTON AND

ALDRIDGE 134^{m}41^c (44^{m}73^c) also S.B.

ALDRIDGE COLLIERY N°2 (LEIGHS WOOD PIT)

Junction 135^{m}37^c

5.Aldridge Colliery Sidings S.B. (45^{m}64^c)

4.Leighs Wood & Aldridge Colliery Co^ys Sidings (45^{m}39^c)

3.Jobern's Aldridge Tileries (45^{m}69^c)

Junction 136^{m}55^c (47^{m}7^c)

End of M.R. 133^{m}75^c

Junction 137^{m}69^c (46^{m}21^c)

WALSALL WOOD 136^{m}39^c (46^{m}71^c)

WALSALL WOOD COLLIERY

Colliery Line Bridge N°15 (47^{m}45^c)

Canal Bridge N°20 (48^{m}7^c)

LOWER STONNALL

M.R. 719

ALDRIDGE COLLIERY N°1

Canal Bridge N°11 (47^{m}77^c)

CANAL AND GOBLIN

WALSALL WOOD

3^{m}54^c

610

50

BRANCH

L. N. W. AND M. R.

LONDON

CANAL

PELSALL

South Staffordshire Junction

Leighs Goods Junction

Norton Junction

Rushall Branch

Wyrley Branch

BLOXWICH

LITTLE BLOXWICH

Hilton Pit

North Walsall Junction 137^{m}15^c (47^{m}63^c)

NORTH WALSALL 137^{m}10^c

See Enlargement

Lichfield Road Junction

Ryecroft Junction

Water Orton Line Junction 137^{m}19^c

Wolverhampton Line Junction 137^{m}15^c

WALSALL PASSENGER STATION 137^{m}63^c

MIDLAND GOODS STATION 138^{m}50^c

See Enlargement

Midland Junction 138^{m}18^c

MIDLAND ENGINE SHED

Pleck Junctions

2^{m}05^c

5^{m}52^c

5^{m}39^c

4^{m}8^c

3^{m}35^c

BLAKENALL HEATH

NORTH WESTERN AND

HOLLY BANK COLLIERY

ESSINGTON COLLIERY

ASHMORE PARK COLLIERY (1913-2)

Reservoir

L. N. W. MOSELEY BRANCH

CANNOCK BRANCH

WYRLEY AND

CANNOCK AND

WEDNESFIELD 141^{m}46^c (52^m)

Whitehall Gas Co^ys Works 139^{m}47^c (49^{m}79^c)

Junction 139^{m}40^c (49^{m}72^c)

Willenhall Junction (50^m)

Stafford S.B. 139^{m}50^c (50^{m}32^c)

Main Siding 138^m (50^{m}59^c)

SHORT HEATH 139^m

WILLENHALL 140^{m}34^c

Station S.B. 140^{m}30^c (50^{m}69^c)

WILLENHALL (L.N.W.)

Portobello Junction

Bentley Canal

Anson Branch Canal

Walsall Canal

Canal

WOLVERHAMPTON See Enlargement

LONDON AND NORTH WESTERN

WALSALL (GOODS)

1^{m}75^c

Priestfield Junction

Portobello Junction

MONMORE GREEN (closed)

L. N. W. GOODS

L. N. W. STATION

G. W. STATION

WOLVERHAMPTON

DUNSTALL PARK

BUSHBURY GOODS STATION

L & N.W. & W. Midland Junction

Bushbury Junction

Aldersley Junction

GRAND JUNCTION

CANAL

From Shrewsbury

From Birmingham

DARLASTON (L. N. W. PASSENGER)

WEDNESBURY L. & N. W. PASSENGER

WOOD GREEN

DARLASTON (GOODS)

Wednesbury Junction

Darlaston Junction

WALSALL JUNCTION

ANSON BRANCH

DARLASTON BRANCH

GREAT BRIDGE

NORTH (G.W. GOODS)

SWAN VILLAGE

WEST BROMWICH

To Birmingham

BESCOT JUNCTION

Bescot Junction L. N. W.

Bescot Sidings L. N. W.

Newton Jc.

NEWTON ROAD (FOR WEST BROMWICH)

GREAT BARR

HAMSTEAD COLLIERY

NORTH GREAT BARR

WESTERN PERRY BARR

To Birmingham

LONDON AND

RUSHALL CANAL

TAME VALLEY

GRAND JUNCTION CANAL

B. C. N.

GREAT WESTERN

BILSTON

DAISY BANK

PRINCES END

BRADLEY AND MOXLEY

DEEPFIELDS AND COSELEY

ETTINGSHALL ROAD AND BILSTON

BLOOMFIELD GOODS

BLOOMFIELD

OCKER HILL

OXFORD WORCESTER AND WOLVERHAMPTON

STOUR VALLEY MAIN LINE

TIPTON L. N. W. STATION

TIPTON G. W. STATION

PRINCES END L. N. W. STATION

DUDLEY PORT (LOW LEVEL)

DUDLEY PORT HIGH LEVEL

DUDLEY L. N. W. STATION

DUDLEY G. W. STATION

ALBION

SEDGLEY

LOWER GORNAL

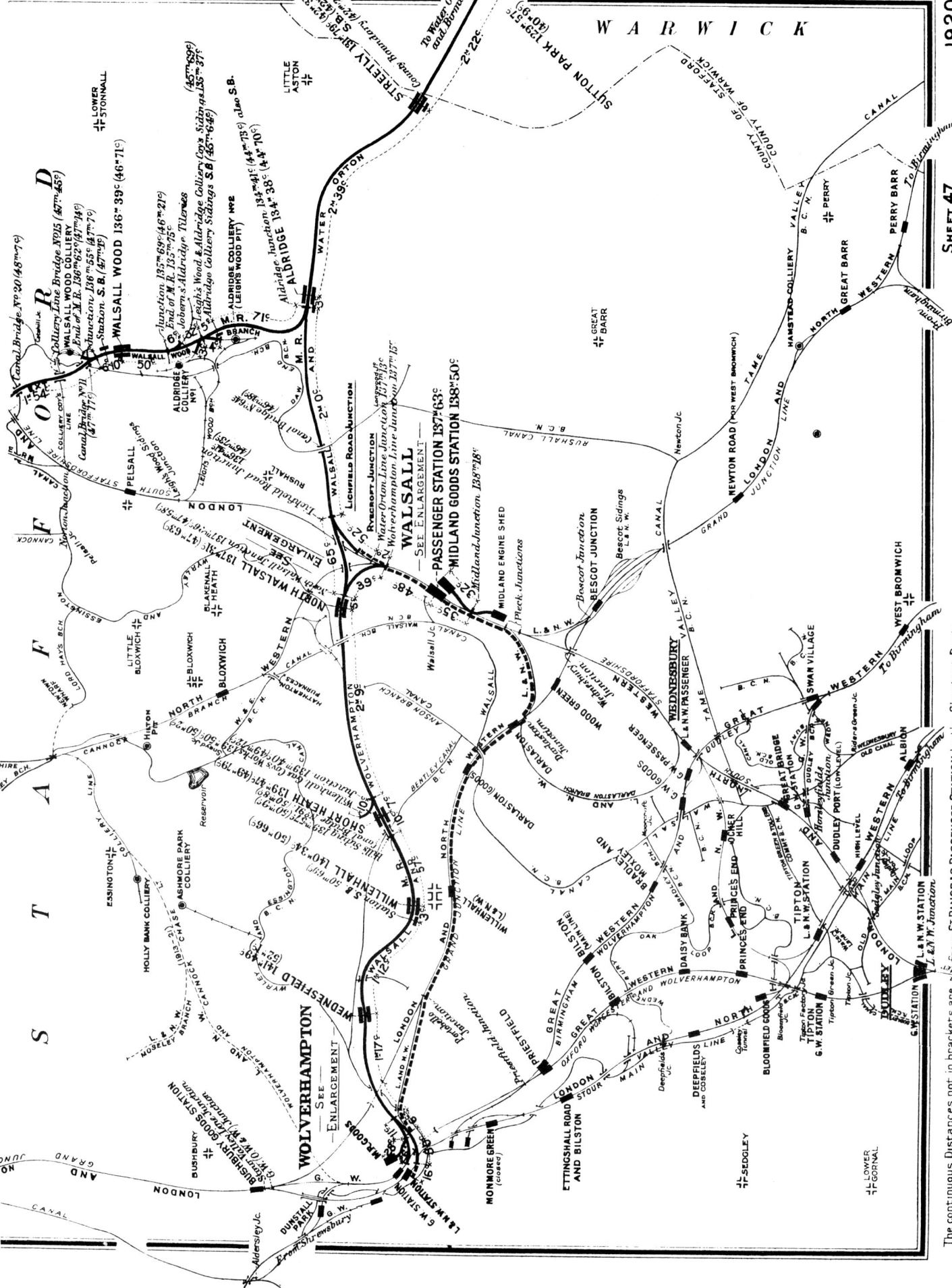

The continuous Distances not in brackets are from St PANCRAS PASSENGER STATION by the Shortest Route.

The continuous Distances in brackets are from London Road Junction, Derby (via Whitacre), and represent the Mile Post Mileage

MIDLAND RAILWAY DISTANCE DIAGRAM, SCALE 1 INCH TO 1 MILE.
NUNEATON DISTRICT.

SHEET 33.

SHEET 25.

SHEET 26.

Sheet 26A.

Book No. 76

(Full-page railway distance diagram of the Nuneaton District. Principal named locations include:)

LEICESTER

MARKET BOSWORTH 119°·43° — Station S.B. 119°·36°
To Ashby

SHENTON 117°·58° — Bosworth Field, Shenton Park

STOKE GOLDING 115°·52° — Station S.B. 115°·58°

HINCKLEY 106°·66° — To Leicester

HIGHAM-ON-THE-HILL 114°·30° — Higham on the Hill 113°·42°

NUNEATON — SEE ENLARGEMENT

Weddington Junction 112°·30° (Via Abbey Junction)
Ashby Junction — Junction of A & N & L & N W Rys 112°·30° (Via Trent Valley Junction)

CHILVERS COTON

Midland Junction

WEDDINGTON JUNCTION — Weddington Junction 112°·43°

COUNTY OF WARWICK / COUNTY OF LEICESTER — BOUNDARY

ASHBY AND NUNEATON JOINT / MIDLAND AND L & N W

ASHBY CANAL

MIDLAND STATION — L & N W STATION

STOCKINGFORD — STOCKINGFORD COLLIERY

HAUNCHWOOD COLLIERY — STOCKINGFORD COLLIERY

End of Stockingford Branch 116°·10°
Green's Siding & End of Rails 115°·46°
Ansley Hall Colliery Branch Junction 115°·70°
ANSLEY HALL COLLIERY

ANSLEY TUNNEL COLLIERY
ARLEY TUNNEL COLLIERY — Tunnel East End, Tunnel West End
ARLEY COLLIERY — Arley Colliery Sidings and S.B.

LOVER WHITACRE — NETHER WHITACRE

WHITACRE — SEE ENLARGEMENT — STATION
Station S.B. 119°·73°
SHUSTOKE 119°·62°
SHUSTOKE — Shustoke Colliery
Station Line Junction
From Birmingham

WHITACRE AND NUNEATON

KINGSBURY — SEE ENLARGEMENT
KINGSBURY STATION JUNCTION
Station Junction S.B. 123°·67°
KINGSBURY 124°·6°
KINGSBURY COLLIERY 123°·9°

Kingsbury Branch Junction S.B. 125°·00°
Kingsbury Branch Junction 124°·77°
BIRCH COPPICE COLLIERY Co
WOODEND PIT No. 3
Junction of Birch Coppice Branch
BIRCH COPPICE COLLIERY No.1 AND 2 PITS
DORDON

End of M.R. 127°·45°

BADDESLEY COLLIERY — BADDESLEY ENSOR
BADDESLEY VIADUCT No. 24
End of M.R. 129°·63°
BAXTERLEY
MEREVALE — Merevale Park
BENTLEY
HURLEY
MANCETTER
ATHERSTONE
WITHERLEY

LONDON AND COVENTRY CANAL AND TRENT
Baddesley Wharf
ANKER RIVER — NORTH VALLEY LINE

GRENDON
POLESWORTH
From Stafford — POLESWORTH
From Derby

AMINGTON COLLIERY
GLASCOTE COLLIERY — GLASCOTE
Glascote Curve South Junction 128°·60°
Perrins & Harrisons Sidings S.B. 128°·8°
Skey's Wilnecote Brick & Works & Colliery 128°·0°
WILNECOTE 127°·59° — Station S.B. 127°·68°
WILNECOTE COLLIERY
Tame Valley Colliery S.B. 127°·7°
TAME VALLEY COLLIERY
Junction 127°·25°
Hinckley Hall Colliery Sidings S.B. 126°·38°
WHATELEY COLLIERY M.R.
The Dosthill Granite Co's S.B.
Cliff Siding — Cliff Sidings S.B. 125°·33°
DOSTHILL

FROM BIRMINGHAM

RIVER SENCE
RIVER TAME
SHEEPY PARVA
RATCLIFFE CULEY
SIBSON
UPTON
WELLSBOROUGH
LATTERTON
FENNY DRAYTON
CALDECOTE

SHEET 33.

1916.

WHITACRE

NUNEATON

COVENTRY

To Rugby

L. & N. W.

TRENT VALLEY LINE

RYTON

BULKINGTON

MARSTON JABBETT

Marston Junction. Junction of Mid. Ry Co's Ashby Canal with the Coventry Canal

EXHALL COLLIERY and Brick Works

WESTERN

GRIFF

BEDWORTH

CHARITY COLLIERY

NEWDIGATES COLLIERY

EXHALL COLLIERY

NORTH

CANAL

COVENTRY BRANCH

HAWKESBURY LANE

Hawkesbury Junction.

L. AND N.W. End of L. & N.W.R.

WYKEN COLLIERY

FOLESHILL

LONGFORD and EXHALL

LONGFORD

Coventry Corporation Gas Works

LITTLE HEATH

BELL GREEN GOODS

Brells Patent Iron Cask Works

GREAT HEATH

RIVER

SOWE

WALSGRAVE ON SOWE

WYKEN

STOKE

COVENTRY LOOP

GOSFORD GREEN GOODS

Three Spires Junction.

KERESLEY

COVENTRY COLLIERY

FOLESHILL

Daimler Motor Works

RADFORD

Rudge Bicycle Works

COUNDON ROAD

COUNDON

COVENTRY

GOODS STATION

PASSENGER STATION L. & N. W.

LONDON AND BIRMINGHAM

Humber Junction

To Rugby

Nuneaton Junction

Leamington Junction

From Birmingham

From Leamington

STIVICHALL

AVON

RIVER

To Hampton

BAGINTON

To Derby

M. R. DERBY & BIRMINGHAM

GOODS YARD

WHITACRE NORTH S.B.

Goods Lines Junction (MEAN) 122 M 19C

Goods Lines Junction 122 M 1C

JUNCTION OF BURTON AND BIRMINGHAM Engineering Districts (31 M 64C)

WHITACRE JUNCTION S.B. 121 M 33C (31 M 67C)

Goods Junction 121 M 40C (31 M 66C)

STATION 121 M 71C (31 M 71C Derby Mileage)

KINGSBURY BRANCH 121 M 39C

Birmingham (via Water Works Siding) 121 M 46C (31 M 78C Hampton Branch)

WHITACRE JUNCTION 121 M 35C (31 M 67C) AND HAMPTON BRANCH (0 M 0C Hampton Branch)

KINGSBURY LINE 121 M 37C (31 M 69C Derby Mileage)

WHITACRE JUNCTION

KESERTON

To Hampton

SHEET 47.

W A R W I C K S H I R E

ARLEY AND FILLONGLEY 117 M 33C (4 M 4C)

Burntwood Bridge

Junction for the Stockingford branch

FILLONGLEY

CURLEY

CORLEY MOOR

COUNDON

Maxstoke Siding 123 M 11C (1 M 32C)

Maxstoke Castle

Station Crossing 123 M 29C (1 M 70C)

COLESHILL 123 M 80C (1 M 71C)

MAXSTOKE

Derby Mileage (0 M 0C Nuneaton Line Mileage)

Junction 121 M 39C (0 M 0C Hampton Branch Mileage) (31 M 71C)

500

Packington Park

STONE BRIDGE

Packington Siding 126 M 22C (4 M 63C)

HAMPTON-IN-ARDEN 127 M 72C (6 M 33C)

Station S.B. 127 M 67C (6 M 28C)

Junction with L. & N.W.R. 128 M 0C (6 M 41C)

HAMPTON BRANCH

2 M 72C

1 M 45C

LITTLE PACKINGTON

L. & N. W. STATION

From Birmingham

To Coventry

HAMPTON

NUNEATON

MERIDEN

To Berkswell & Carlisle

Weddington Junction 112 M 43C (Via Abbey Junction)

Weddington Junction S.B. 112 M 42C

WEDDINGTON JUNCTION

ASHBY JUNCTION

Ashby Junction S.B. 112 M 33C

Ashby Junction (A & N. Line with L & N.W.) 112 M 30C via Trent Valley Mid. Junction

Trent Valley Junction 112 M 43C (Via Abbey Junction)

TRENT VALLEY JUNCTION, Mid. with L. & N. W.

Trent Valley Junction, Mid. with L. & N.W. 112 M 30C

Trent Valley Mid. Junction

112 M 13C (10 M 14C Ex Whitacre Junction)

Coventry Canal Bridge No 33. 112 M 30C (9 M 29C Ex Whitacre Junc.)

Custom Road Crossing (10 M 71C)

Nuneaton South S.B. 110 M 72C (11 M 30C) with Mid.

Midland Junction S.B. 110 M 75C (11 M 32C Ex Whitacre) Junction

MIDLAND JUNCTION

MIDLAND LINE

To Leicester

ASHBY AND NUNEATON JOINT L. AND N. W.

From Lichfield

TRENT VALLEY LINE L. & N. W.

COVENTRY LINE

N.W.R. BRIDGE No 2 112 M 12C

From Birmingham

Judkins Siding Junction

A & N. Junction S.B. 111 M 76C

A & N. Line with Mid. Ry 112 M 7C

L. & N. W.R. BRIDGE No 1

Tuttle Hill Quarries

TUTTLE HILL QUARRIES

MIDLAND GOODS YARD

Midland Junction S.B. 111 M 56C (9 M 54C)

ABBEY JUNCTION 111 M 56C (9 M 54C)

Loop Line Junction 111 M 66C (9 M 59C)

Abbey Junction S.B. 111 M 56C

MIDLAND STATION (ABBEY STREET) 111 M 67C (9 M 50C)

Station S.B. 111 M 62C (9 M 50C)

ABBEY STREET

ASHBY AND NUNEATON J.

Via Ashby Junction

NUNEATON

L. & N. W. BRIDGE S.B. 111 M 23C (10 M 8C)

Nuneaton Bridge S.B.

Nuneaton Siding S.B. 111 M 53C (9 M 64C)

Trent Valley Junction 112 M 45C Via Abbey Junction 112 M 42C

Via Whitacre Junction

No 1 S.B.

No 2 S.B.

L. AND N. W. STATION 112 M 4C (10 M 15C)

L. & N. W.

Leicester Line Junction

LEICESTERSHIRE LINE

Coventry Line Junction

L. & N.W. ENGINE SHED

ANKER MILL

To Rugby

From Coventry

To Rugby

The continuous Distances not in brackets are from ST. PANCRAS PASSENGER STATION by the Shortest Route.

The continuous Distances in brackets represent the Mile Post Mileage.

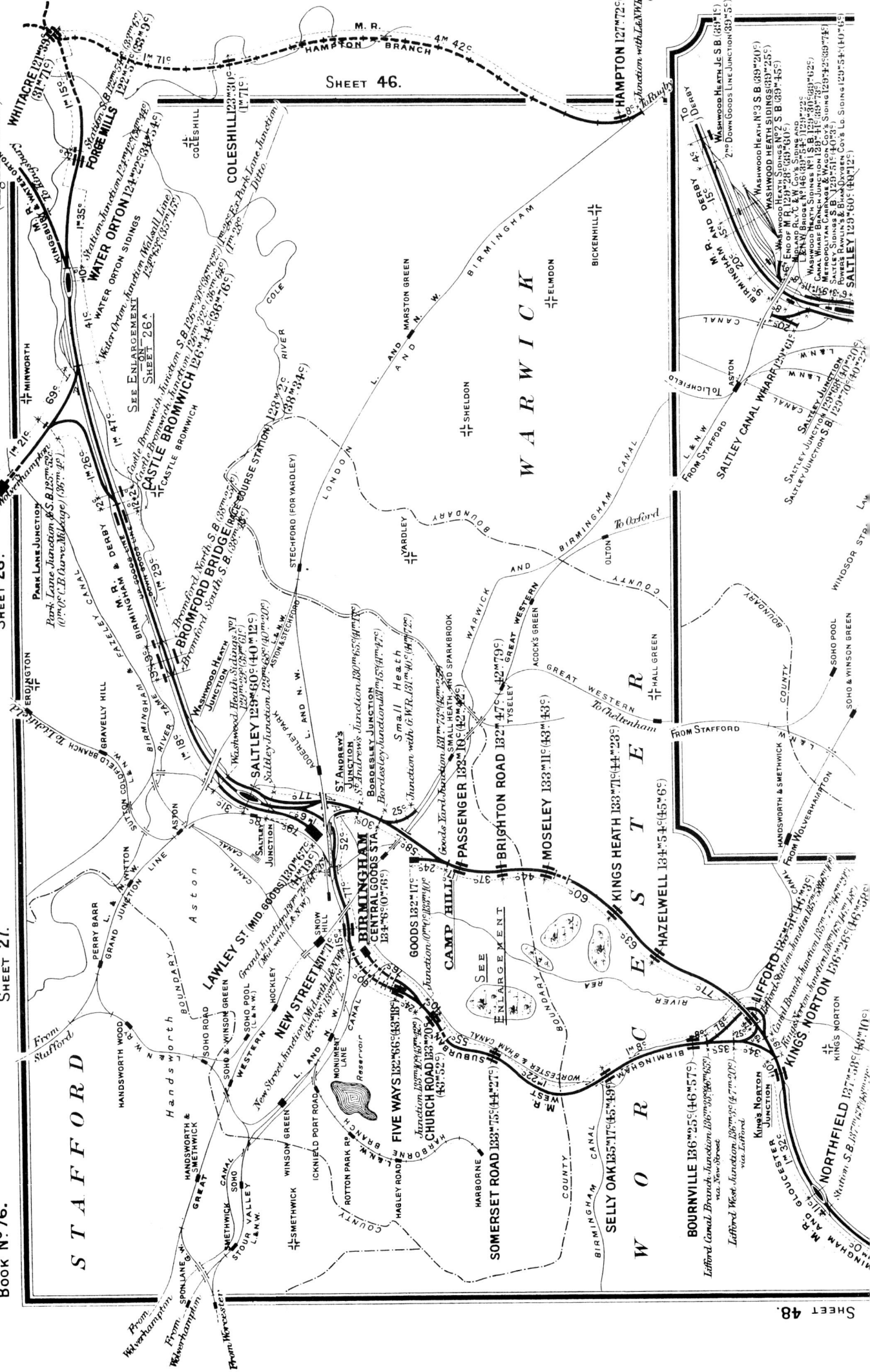

MIDLAND RAILWAY DISTANCE DIAGRAM. SCALE 1 INCH TO 1 MILE.
(BIRMINGHAM AND DISTRICT.)

(Eighth Edition.)

SHEET 47.

SHEET 26A.

SHEET 27.

BOOK No. 76.

SHEET 46.

M.R.

HAMPTON BRANCH   4M 42C

WHITACRE 121M 59C

FORGE MILLS

WATER ORTON 124M 22C

WATER ORTON SIDINGS

COLESHILL 123M 31C

PENNS (GOODS) 126M 73C (37M 2C)

MINWORTH

See Enlargement SHEET 26A

CASTLE BROMWICH 126M 44C (66M 16C)

BROMFORD BRIDGE

WARWICK

BICKENHILL

ELMDON

MARSTON GREEN

SHELDON

BIRMINGHAM

L. AND N.W.

YARDLEY

STECHFORD (FOR YARDLEY)

WASHWOOD HEATH

SALTLEY 129M 60C (40M 12C)

SALTLEY JUNCTION

COLE

RIVER

HAMPTON 127M 72C (6M 33C)

To Rugby

To Derby

M.R. AND DERBY

WASHWOOD HEATH No.3 S.B. (39M 20C)
WASHWOOD HEATH No.2 S.B. (39M 45C)
WASHWOOD HEATH SIDINGS (39M 25C)

SALTLEY

SALTLEY CANAL WHARF

SALTLEY JUNCTION 129M 70C

ASTON

To Lichfield

From Stafford

CANAL

L. & N.W.

PERRY BARR

GRAND JUNCTION

ERDINGTON

GRAVELLY HILL

SUTTON COLDFIELD BRANCH TO LICHFIELD

HANDSWORTH WOOD

SOHO ROAD

SOHO & WINSON GREEN

WESTERN

GREAT

SMETHWICK

STOUR VALLEY L.&N.W.

HANDSWORTH & SMETHWICK

SOHO

HANDSWORTH

BOUNDARY

ASTON

ADDERLEY PARK

St. ANDREW'S JUNCTION

BORDESLEY JUNCTION

SMALL HEATH

Small Heath AND SPARKBROOK

GREAT WESTERN

ACOCK'S GREEN

To Cheltenham

HALL GREEN

OLTON

To Oxford

LAWLEY ST. (MID. GOODS)

NEW STREET STATION

BIRMINGHAM CENTRAL GOODS STA.

HOCKLEY

SNOW HILL

MONUMENT LANE

Reservoir

ICKNIELD PORT ROAD

ROTTON PARK ROAD

HARBORNE BRANCH L.&N.W.

HAGLEY ROAD

HARBORNE

FIVE WAYS 132M 66C (43M 18C)

CHURCH ROAD 132M 70C

SOMERSET ROAD 133M 15C (44M 17C)

WINSON GREEN

SOHO POOL

SUBURBAN

WORCESTER & BHAM CANAL

BIRMINGHAM WEST M.R.

CAMP HILL

PASSENGER 132M 10C

GOODS 132M 17C

BRIGHTON ROAD 132M 47C (42M 79C)

TYSELEY

MOSELEY 133M 11C (43M 43C)

KINGS HEATH 133M 71C (44M 23C)

HAZELWELL 134M 51C (45M 6C)

SELLY OAK 135M 17C (45M 49C)

BOURNVILLE 136M 25C (46M 57C)

RIVER REA

SEE ENLARGEMENT

STECHFORD

KINGS NORTON

LIFFORD 135M 45C

KINGS NORTON JUNCTION

NORTHFIELD 137M 50C

M.R. AND GLOUCESTER

WORCESTER

STAFFORD

WARWICK

WORCESTER

From Stafford

From Wolverhampton

From Worcester

SHEET 48.

ENLARGEMENT OF BIRMINGHAM AND DISTRICT.

1913.

SHEET 49.

(THOS KELL & SON, LONDON.)

W A R W I C K

W O R C E S T E R

Small Heath

Edgbaston

Bournbrook

Metchley

TO OXFORD

TYSELEY

GREAT WESTERN

From Wolverhampton

CANAL

GREAT WESTERN

LAND & N.W.

Winson Green

Monument Lane

Hockley

Rotton Park Rd

Hagley Rd

ICKNIELD PORT Rd

MR. & LAND N.W.

Station labels and junctions (top to bottom, left group)

SALTLEY JUNCTION 129°68°(40°20°)
SALTLEY JUNCTION S.B. 129°70°(40°22°)
ENGINE SHED JUNCTION 130°8°(40°40°)
DUDDESTON ROAD JUNCTION S.B. 130°9° (40°41°) TO STECHFORD
SALTLEY ENGINE SHEDS
LANDOR STREET JUNCTION
LANDOR STREET JUNCTION 130°26° (40°58°)
LANDOR STREET JUNCTION S.B. 130°32°(40°64°)
MIDLAND CARRIAGE & WAGON COY'S SIDING 130°35°
L & N.W. BRIDGE N°157 (40°75°)
ST. ANDREW'S JUNCTION
ST. ANDREW'S JUNCTION 130°65° (41°17°) S.B. 130°75°(0°10°)
BRICKYARD CROSSING AND S.B. 130°+ (41°41°0°)
MIDLAND FUEL COY & BATCHELOR'S SIDING 130°75° (0°10°)
BORDESLEY JUNCTION (0°0° CURVE MILEAGE)
BORDESLEY JUNCTION S.B. 131°+ (41°47°)
BORDESLEY JUNCTION 131°15°(41°47°)
BORDESLEY JUNCTION S.B. 131°17° (41°49°)
JUNCTION OF MID. AND G.W. 131°+(41°72°)

SUDDESTON SIDING
SHEET ST. S.B. (40°34°)
WHARF L & N.W.
LAWLEY STREET B° S.B. (41°11°)
LAWLEY STREET GOODS 130°6° (41°11°)
GRAND JUNCTION S.B. 130°+(41°11°)
GLOUCESTER LINES WITH L & N.W.(40°65°)
(EX. LONDON & N.W. JOINT)
JUNCTION FOUR FOUR ST. ANDREW'S (DERBY)
JUNCTION OF MID. & L.W.J.(130°)+(41°)
CURZON ST. S.B. 131°7°(41°11°)
SNOW HILL 131°7° (42°39°)
SOUTH TUNNEL 131°
L & N.W. GOODS

CAMP HILL
GOODS YARD JUNCTION 131°+(42°23°)
STATION S.B. 131°44°(42°26°)
PASSENGER 132°10°(42°42°)

BRIGHTON ROAD 132°24° (42°79°)
STATION S.B. 132°53° (42°25°)

MOSELEY 133°11°(43°43°)
MOSELEY TUNNEL (166 YARDS) N°141 (NORTH END 43°47°) (SOUTH END 43°54°)

KING'S HEATH 133°69°(44°21°)
STATION S.B. 133°71°(44°23°)

HAZELWELL 134°54°(45°6°)
STATION S.B. 134°60°(45°12°)

LIFFORD CANAL WHARF 136°40°

SMALL HEATH AND SPARKBROOK
HIGHGATE COAL WHARF
NADIN & ELLIS COAL SIDING.
STATION COY'S SIDING.

BORDESLEY SIDINGS (G.W.R.)

COUNTY BOUNDARY (43°18°)

Left-centre group

WHARF WESTERN
GREAT HOCKLEY
LAND N.W.

NEW STREET STATION (L & N.W. AND MID JOINT)
JUNCTION OF MID. AND WEST SUBURBAN
WITH L & N.W. 132°+(42°88°)
NEW STREET
JUNCTION

SUFFOLK ST. TUNNEL 176 YDS N°1 132°+
CANAL TUNNEL 224 YDS N°3
GRANVILLE ST. TUNNEL 83 YDS N°4
BATH ROW TUNNEL 209 YDS N°5
CENTRAL GOODS STATION
BIRMINGHAM CENTRAL S.B. 132°+
GRANVILLE ST. GOODS TUNNEL 234 YDS
BIRMINGHAM CORP. TUNNEL 108 YDS
BATH ROW GOODS TUNNEL
GOODS 132°42°(0°12°)
JUNCTION 132°+(0°0°)
FIVE WAYS 132°68°(43°18°)
CHURCH ROAD 133°20°(43°52°)
CENTRAL GOODS STA BRANCH JUNC. 132°
CENTRAL GOODS STA. BRANCH JUNCTION 133°10°(0°0°)

CHURCH RD TUNNEL N°10 107 YARDS
(43°55° AND 43°60°)

SOMERSET ROAD 133°65°(43°97°)
(FOR HARBORNE)

HARBORNE

BIRMINGHAM WEST SUBURBAN M.R.

COUNTY BOUNDARY (45°19°)

COUNTY BOUNDARY (45°39°)

VIADUCT N°20 (45°39°)

SELLY OAK 135°17°(45°49°)
STATION S.B. 135°30°(45°62°)

PATENT ENAMEL COY'S SIDING 135°44°

CANAL BRIDGE N°45 (45°74°)
CADBURY'S SIDINGS JUNCTION 135°71°(46°23°)
GEO. CADBURY'S SIDING 135°79°(46°31°)

BOURNVILLE 136°17°(46°49°)
CADBURY'S CHOCOLATE WORKS 136°17°(46°57°)
CANAL BRANCH JUNCTION 136°33°(46°65°)
STATION S.B. (46°71°)
STRACHLEY STREET ENGINE SHED

WORCESTER & BHAM CANAL

CANAL BRANCH

LIFFORD WEST JUNCTION
LIFFORD WEST JUNCTION 136°3° VIA LIFFORD (47°20°)
WEST JUNCTION S.B. 136°13°(47°22°)

LIFFORD 135°51°(46°93°)
LIFFORD STATION JUNCTION
LIFFORD STATION JUNCTION S.B. 135°82°(46°14°)
NEW METAL COY'S SIDING
LIFFORD 136°17°(47°58°)
LIFFORD CANAL BRANCH JUNCTION

KING'S NORTON JUNCTION 136°18°(46°49°) VIA CAMP HILL
KING'S NORTON JUNCTION 135°58°(46°10°) VIA CAMP HILL
KING'S NORTON JUNCTION S.B. 135°82°(46°14°) VIA LIFFORD CANAL BRANCH
GOODS JUNCTION S.B. 136°19° VIA NEW STREET
KING'S NORTON CANAL BRANCH

KING'S NORTON JUNCTION 135°77°(46°9°) VIA CAMP HILL
GOODS JUNCTION 136°26°(47°54°) VIA NEW STREET
GOODS LINES JUNCTION S.B. 136°33°(47°88°)
KING'S NORTON SIDINGS (47°99°)

KING'S NORTON
STATION 136°3° VIA LIFFORD
GOODS JUNCTION S.B. 136°19°(47°22°)
KING'S NORTON CANAL BRANCH JUNCTION 136°33°(46°67°)
PERSHORE ROAD TUNNEL (N°35) (60 YARDS)
(47°33°–47°36°)

FROM GLOUCESTER
UP GOODS
FROM GLOUCESTER

Left section (separate lower map)

From Halesowen
G.W. AND M.R.
HALESOWEN JUNCTION
HALESOWEN BRANCH JUNCTION 138°62°(41°30°)
HALESOWEN JUNCTION S.B. 138°63° (41°45°)
COFTON TUNNEL N°120 (44°50°)
440 YARDS (44°70°)

COSTON JUNCTION
HACKETT G.W. AND M.R.

WEST HILL

WEST HILL TUNNEL

BIRMINGHAM

HOPWOOD

Upper Bittell Reservoir
Lower Bittell Reservoir

BARNT GREEN JUNCTION
Main Line Junction S.B. 141°5°(57°57°)
Main Line Junction 141°+(57°58°)
BARNT GREEN 141°5°(57°57°)
Single Line Junction 141°+(57°+)
Junction S.B. (57°+)

ALVECHURCH 143°11°(53°46°)

ROWNEY GREEN

FORHILL

WYTHALL

WEATHEROAK

BEDLEY

FROM WOLVERHAMPTON

From Gloucester

Lower Redditch section

REDDITCH
Redditch Gas Light Coy's Siding 146°+
T.& M. Dixon's Gas Wharf 146°5°
Junction of Redditch & Evesham & Redditch Sidings S.B.
North S.B. 146°3°
South S.B. 146°+
REDDITCH TUNNEL (N°23) 340 YARDS
STATION 146°33°(55°65°)

River Arrow

REDDITCH BRANCH M.R.

EVESHAM AND REDDITCH M.R.

STUDLEY & ASTWOOD BANK 149°+(57°79°)
Station S.B. 149°47°(61°78°)

HEADLESS CROSS
CRABBS CROSS
IPSLEY
ASTWOOD BANK
STUDLEY

To Evesham

To Evesham

WORCESTER
COBLEY

BOUNDARY
COUNTY

Footnote

The continuous Distances not in brackets are from St. Pancras Passenger Station by the Shortest Route.

The continuous Distances in brackets represent the Mile Post Mileage (New) from Trafford Park Junction, Derby, via Whitacre.

MIDLAND RAILWAY DISTANCE DIAGRAM. SCALE 1 INCH TO 1 MILE.

BROMSGROVE DISTRICT.

SHEET **48.**
(Sixth Edition.)

SHEET 47.

SHEET 27.

SHEET 27.

BOOK No. 76

WARWICK

STAFFORD

To Birmingham

To Birmingham

SMETHWICK

SMETHWICK

From Wolverhampton

WEST BROMWICH

SPON LANE

SMETHWICK JUNCTION STA:

LANGLEY GREEN AND ROOD END

ALBION

OLDBURY

OLDBURY

ROWLEY REGIS AND BLACKHEATH

ROWLEY REGIS

WINDMILL END

DARBY END HALT

BLACKHEATH

HIGH ST HALT

OLD HILL

HIGH LEVEL

To Wolverhampton

From Wolverhampton

DUDLEY

G.W. PASSENGER

L & N.W. GOODS

G.W. & L.N.W. Junction

L.& N.W. Junction

NETHERTON

BAPTIST END HALT

NETHERTON

WITHYMOOR GOODS

OLD HILL GOODS

CRADLEY HEATH

WITLEY COLLIERY

CRADLEY COLLIERY

LYE

JUNCTION STATION

STOURBRIDGE

TOWN

NETHERTON TUNNEL

CANAL TUNNEL

WESTERN TUNNEL

GREAT WESTERN

GREAT WESTERN

GORNAL WOOD

HARTSHILL & WOODSIDE

ROUND OAK

BRIERLEY HILL

Kingswinford Junction

BRETTELL LANE

SWINDON

KINGSWINFORD

From Wolverhampton

STAFFORDSHIRE AND WORCESTERSHIRE CANAL

WORDSLEY

WOLLASTON

KINVER

RIVER STOUR

COUNTY

BOUNDARY

CHURCHILL

CHURCHILL AND BLAKEDOWN

BROOM

HAGLEY

HAGLEY

PEDMORE

HASBURY

HALESOWEN

CLENT HILLS
▲1036

CLENT

ROMSLEY

Wolverley

WESTERN RAILWAY

600

700

QUINTON BOUNDARY

Coombes Holloway Halt

Halesowen Canal Basin

STATION 14.4.M 63C.
South S.B. 14.4.M 82C.

End of Joint Line 14.M.59C (5.M 70C)

HUNNINGTON 142.M 74F (41.5F)

LAPAL TUNNEL

BIRMINGHAM, OR DUDLEY CANAL

BARTLEY GREEN

ILLEY

FRANKLEY, OR DOWERY DELL VIADUCT No 10: (31.M 41.F)

FRANKLEY

HALESOWEN BRANCH

(G.W. AND M. JOINT)

1.M 65C

1.M 18C

1.M 12C

1.M 14C

HALESOWEN

RUBERY

Holly Hill Crossing (Mo:36) West (1.M 33.5)

Halesowen Junction S.B. (M.o:44) Loop Siding (1.M 38)

Junction with (Mo Birmingham Central Goods) Sidings (1.M 18)

50.60

Halesowen Junction S.B. (1.M 0:43) Loop (Mo:69)

(Goods Lines Junction (48.M 20C)
Branch Junction 138.M 69F (49.M 21F)

To Birmingham

NORTHFIELD
137.M 58F (48.M 10F *)

WEST TRAMWAY

Frogs Mill Siding Crossing (1.M 52)

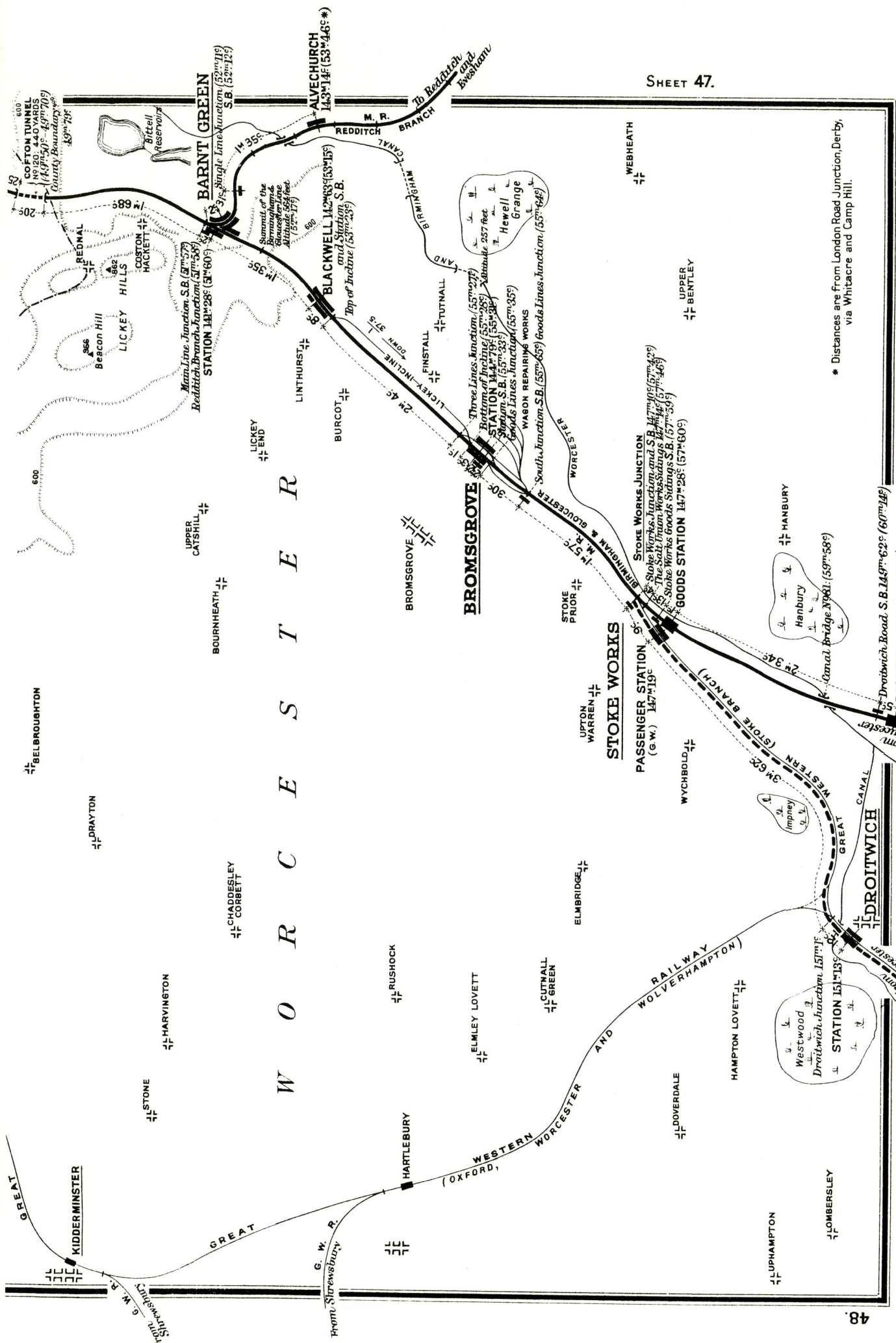

1914.

BARNT GREEN (52m.71c) (52m.12c)

ALVECHURCH 143m.14c (53m.46c *)

To Redditch and Evesham

M.R.

REDDITCH BRANCH

COFTON TUNNEL No 120 440 YARDS ((149m.50c-149m.70c)) County Boundary (49m.79c)

Bittell Reservoirs

600

589

1m.35c

2¾c Single Line Junction (52m..) S.B.

Summit of the Birmingham & Gloucester Line Altitude 564 feet (52m.17c)

BLACKWELL 142m.63c (53m.15c) and Station S.B. (53m.23c)

Main Line Junction S.B. (51m.57c) Redditch Branch Junction (51m.58c) STATION 141m.28c (51m.60c)

REDNAL

COSTON HACKETT

LICKEY HILLS

862

Beacon Hill 956

600

Top of Incline

LINTHURST

LICKEY END

BURCOT

DOWN 37·5

2m.4c

LICKEY INCLINE

BIRMINGHAM AND GLOUCESTER

FINSTALL

TUTNALL

Three Lines Junction (55m.27c) Bottom of Incline (55m.28c) Altitude 257 feet STATION 144m.79c (55m.31c) Station S.B. (55m.33c) Goods Lines Junction (55m.35c)

WAGON REPAIRING WORKS

South Junction S.B. (55m.55c) Goods Lines Junction (55m.64c)

Hewell Grange

WEBHEATH

UPPER BENTLEY

1m.57c M.R.

BIRMINGHAM & GLOUCESTER

WORCESTER

BROMSGROVE

UPPER CATSHILL

BOURNHEATH

BROMSGROVE

STOKE PRIOR

Stoke Works Junction and S.B. 147m.10c (57m.42c) The Salt Union Works Sidings 147m.19c (57m.46c) STATION 147m.28c (57m.59c) Stoke Works Goods Sidings S.B. (57m.60c)

GOODS STATION 147m.28c (57m.60c)

HANBURY

Hanbury

Canal Bridge No 61 (59m.58c)

STOKE WORKS PASSENGER STATION (G.W.) 147m.19c

UPTON WARREN

WYCHBOLD

GREAT WESTERN (STOKE BRANCH)

3m.62c

Droitwich Road S.B. 149m.62c (60m.14c) DROITWICH ROAD (GOODS) 149m.67c (60m.19c) *

From Gloucester

GREAT

CANAL

ELMBRIDGE

CUTNALL GREEN

Impney

HAMPTON LOVETT

DOVERDALE

OMBERSLEY

UPHAMPTON

RUSHOCK

CHADDESLEY CORBETT

DRAYTON

BELBROUGHTON

STONE

HARVINGTON

W O R C E S T E R

GREAT WESTERN RAILWAY (OXFORD, WORCESTER AND WOLVERHAMPTON)

HARTLEBURY

G.W.R.

From Shrewsbury

KIDDERMINSTER

GREAT WESTERN

DROITWICH

Droitwich Junction 151m.7c STATION 151m.13c

From Worcester

Westwood

* Distances are from London Road Junction, Derby, via Whitacre and Camp Hill.

The continuous Distances not in brackets are from St Pancras Passenger Station by the Shortest Route.

The continuous Distances in brackets represent the Mile Post Mileage.

MIDLAND RAILWAY DISTANCE DIAGRAM. SCALE 1 INCH TO 1 MILE.
(ALCESTER–EVESHAM–ASHCHURCH.)

BOOK No 76

SHEET 49.
(Fifth Edition.)

SHEET 47.

SHEET 50.

To Bearley

ASTON CANTLOW

GREAT ALNE

GREAT WESTERN RAILWAY
(ALCESTER AND BEARLEY BRANCH)

KINWARTON

TEMPLE GRAFTON

To Stratford-on-Avon
and Obney BINTON

DORSINGTON

RIVER ARROW

STUDLEY & ASTWOOD BANK 149ᴹ 47ᶜ (59ᴹ 79ᶜ)

From Redditch

SAMBOURN

COUGHTON 151ᴹ 62ᶜ (62ᴹ 14ᶜ)

Coughton Park

Loop Junction North 153ᴹ 44ᶜ (63ᴹ 76ᶜ)
Alcester Junction S.B. 153ᴹ 46ᶜ (63ᴹ 78ᶜ)
Alcester Junction 153ᴹ 48ᶜ (64ᴹ 0ᶜ)
ALCESTER STATION 153ᴹ 68ᶜ (64ᴹ 20ᶜ)
Station S.B. (64ᴹ 21ᶜ)
Loop Junction South 153ᴹ 73ᶜ (64ᴹ 25ᶜ)

ARROW

LEXHALL

Arrow Bridge Nᵒ 45 (65ᴹ 1ᶜ)
Arrow Bridge Nᵒ 48 (66ᴹ 4ᶜ)

WIXFORD 155ᴹ 66ᶜ (66ᴹ 18ᶜ)

WEETHLEY

Ragley Park

WARWICK

WORCESTER

Loop Junction North (68ᴹ 69ᶜ)
North S.B. 156ᴹ 38ᶜ (66ᴹ 70ᶜ)
BROOM JUNCTION JOINT STATION 156ᴹ 43ᶜ (86ᴹ 75ᶜ)
South S.A. and S.& M. Junction Ry. Junction 156ᴹ 48ᶜ (67ᴹ 0ᶜ)
Loop Junction South (67ᴹ 4ᶜ)
STRATFORD-ON-AVON AND MIDLAND JUNCTION RY
(EVESHAM REDDITCH AND STRATFORD-ON-AVON SECTION)
BIDFORD-ON-AVON

BIDFORD

DUNNINGTON

RIVER AVON

Junction 157ᴹ 65ᶜ (68ᴹ 11ᶜ)
Bomford & Eversheds Siding 157ᴹ 6?ᶜ (68ᴹ ?9ᶜ)
SALFORD PRIORS 157ᴹ 74ᶜ (68ᴹ 26ᶜ)
County Boundary (68ᴹ 51ᶜ)

SALFORD PRIORS

ABBOTS SALFORD

County Boundary (68ᴹ 66ᶜ)

CLEEVE PRIOR

RIVER AVON

Station S.B. 159ᴹ 70ᶜ (70ᴹ 22ᶜ)
HARVINGTON 159ᴹ 75ᶜ (70ᴹ 27ᶜ)
County Boundary (69ᴹ 68ᶜ)

HARVINGTON

FECKENHAM

BRADLEY

DORMSTON

INKBERROW

ABBOTS MORTON

ROUS LENCH

ABBOTS LENCH

CHURCH LENCH

KINGTON

FLYFORD FLAVELL

FLADBURY (LABBERTON)

BISHAMPTON

THROCKMORTON

GRAFTON FLYFORD

NORTH PIDDLE

NAUNTON BEAUCHAMP

COWSDEN

PINVIN

From Worcester

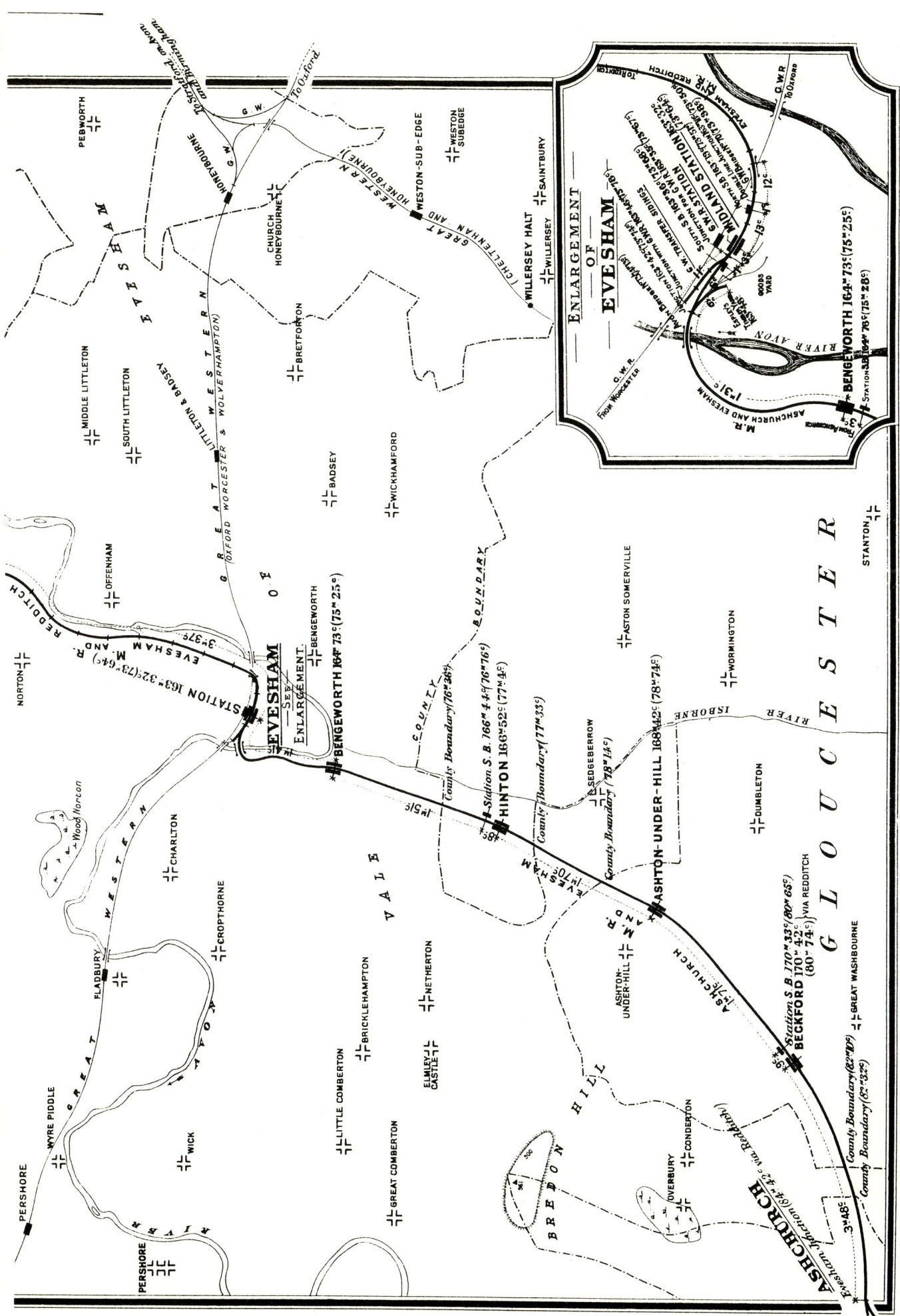

1912.

ENLARGEMENT
OF
EVESHAM

To Redditch

EVESHAM AND REDDITCH

G.W.R.
To Oxford

MIDLAND STATION

G.W.R. STATION

South S.B.
G.W. TRANSFER SIDINGS

GOODS YARD

From Worcester
G.W.R.

RIVER AVON

M.R. ASHCHURCH AND EVESHAM

Station S.B.
From Ashchurch

BENGEWORTH 164·73ᶜ (75·25ᶜ)
Station S.B. 164·76ᶜ (75·28ᶜ)

To Stratford on Avon
and Birmingham

G.W.
To Oxford

G.W.

HONEYBOURNE

GREAT WESTERN

CHELTENHAM AND HONEYBOURNE

CHURCH HONEYBOURNE

WESTON-SUB-EDGE
WESTON SUBEDGE

WILLERSEY HALT
WILLERSEY
SAINTBURY

BRETFORTON

PEBWORTH

MIDDLE LITTLETON

SOUTH LITTLETON

LITTLETON & BADSEY

GREAT WESTERN
(OXFORD WORCESTER & WOLVERHAMPTON)

BADSEY

WICKHAMFORD

OF

EVESHAM
See ENLARGEMENT.

BENGEWORTH

OFFENHAM

NORTON

R. AND REDDITCH
EVESHAM AND M.
3·37ᶜ

STATION 163·32ᶜ (73·64ᶜ)

BENGEWORTH 164·73ᶜ (75·25ᶜ)

COUNTY BOUNDARY

County Boundary (76·36ᶜ)

Station S.B. 166·44ᶜ (76·76ᶜ)
HINTON 166·52ᶜ (77·4ᶜ)

County Boundary (77·33ᶜ)

SEDGEBERROW
County Boundary (78·14ᶜ)

ASTON SOMERVILLE

WICK

GREAT COMBERTON

LITTLE COMBERTON

ELMLEY CASTLE

NETHERTON

BRICKLEHAMPTON

CHARLTON

CROPTHORNE

FLADBURY

Wood Norton

VALE

WYRE PIDDLE

PERSHORE

PERSHORE

RIVER AVON

GREAT WESTERN

EVESHAM

RIVER ISBORNE

ASHTON-UNDER-HILL 168·42ᶜ (78·74ᶜ)

DUMBLETON

WORMINGTON

STANTON

ASHTON-UNDER-HILL

EVESHAM AND M.R.
1·70ᶜ

ASHCHURCH
1·77ᶜ

Station S.B. 170·33ᶜ (80·65ᶜ)
BECKFORD 170·42ᶜ (80·74ᶜ) } VIA REDDITCH

GREAT WASHBOURNE

County Boundary (82·11ᶜ)
County Boundary (82·32ᶜ)

CONDERTON

OVERBURY

BREDON HILL

ASHCHURCH (84·42ᶜ) via Redditch

Evesham Junction (84·48ᶜ) via Redditch

3·48ᶜ

GLOUCESTER

The continuous Distances not in Brackets are from St Pancras Passenger Station by the Shortest Route.

The continuous Distances in Brackets are from London Road Junction, Derby, via Whitacre, Camp Hill, & Redditch, and represent the Mile Post Mileage (New).

MIDLAND RAILWAY DISTANCE DIAGRAM. SCALE 1 INCH TO 1 MILE.
WORCESTER DISTRICT.

SHEET 50.
(Fifth Edition.)

BOOK No. 76

To Birmingham

SHEET 48.

DROITWICH ROAD 149ᴹ67ᶜ (GOODS) (60ᴹ19ᶜ EX LONDON Rᴰ JUNCTION DERBY VIA WHITACRE)

DROITWICH 151ᴹ13ᶜ

DUNHAMPSTEAD (GOODS) 151ᴹ59ᶜ and Crossing & S.B. (62ᴹ11ᶜ)

Oddingley Crossing & S.B. 62ᴹ59ᶜ

HADZOR

HIMBLETON

1ᴹ72ᶜ

48ᶜ

MARTIN HUSSINGTREE

HUDDINGTON

CROWLE GREEN

CROWLE

FERNHILL HEATH 154ᴹ13ᶜ

Hindlip Park

BREDICOT

BROUGHTON HACKETT

UPTON SNODSBURY 155ᴹ65ᶜ (66ᴹ17ᶜ) S.B. (66ᴹ16ᶜ)

SPETCHLEY (GOODS) 155ᴹ62ᶜ

M. R. AND

BIRMINGHAM

TIBBERTON

WARNDON

Spetchley Trees Sandhu 155ᴹ24ᶜ

WHITE LADIES ASTON

PEOPLETON

Norton Crossing & S.B. 67ᴹ31ᶜ

G.W. Bridge No 19ᴬ (68ᴹ45ᶜ)

Junction of Birmingham & Gloucester Engineering Districts (68ᴹ53ᶜ)

GREAT WESTERN WORCESTER & WOLVERHAMPTON

To Oxford

(OXFORD, WORCESTER & WOLVERHAMPTON)

Junction of Birmingham & Gloucester Junction (Mid. with G.W.) 158ᴹ27ᶜ (68ᴹ59ᶜ) S.B. (68ᴹ60ᶜ)

Abbot's Wood Junction

STOULTON

DRAKE'S BROUGHTON

WADBOROUGH 159ᴹ17ᶜ (69ᴹ79ᶜ)

Station Crossing (70ᴹ29ᶜ)

AND

GLOUCESTER

WHITTINGTON

Norton Junction & S.B. 158ᴹ8ᶜ

3ᴹ38ᶜ

1ᴹ34ᶜ

4ᴹ5ᶜ

38ᶜ

9ᶜ

1ᴹ20ᶜ

HATFIELD

Abbot's Wood Junction

NORTON

STONEHALL

NORTON JUNCTION STATION 159ᴹ13ᶜ VIA ABBOTS WOOD JUNCTION Norton Junction & S.B. 158ᴹ8ᶜ

GREAT WESTERN

2ᴹ45ᶜ

59ᶜ

7ᶜ

CLAINES

To Birmingham

WORCESTER AND BIRMINGHAM CANAL (NAVIGATION)

WORCESTER AND BIRMINGHAM CANAL

DROITWICH CANAL

50ᶜ

3ᴹ0ᶜ

GREAT WESTERN

2ᴹ13ᶜ

Junction of Joint Station Lines North 156ᴹ26ᶜ

Tunnel Junction 156ᴹ25ᶜ

28ᶜ

WORCESTER — SEE ENLARGEMENT —

Shrub Hill Junction 156ᴹ56ᶜ

SHRUB HILL PASSENGER STATION 156ᴹ62ᶜ (G.W. AND MID. JOINT)

MIDLAND GOODS STATION 157ᴹ9ᶜ

Junction of Joint Station Lines South 157ᴹ1ᶜ

6ᶜ

27ᶜ

15ᶜ

KEMPSEY

SEVERN

Rainbow Hill Junction 156ᴹ56ᶜ

FOREGATE STREET 157ᴹ6ᶜ

32ᶜ

30ᶜ

17ᶜ

54ᶜ

ST. JOHN'S

LOWER WICK

POWICK

CALLOW END

HENWICK 157ᴹ60ᶜ

UPPER WICK

Leominster Junction 160ᴹ72ᶜ

BRANSFORD ROAD 160ᴹ37ᶜ

COTHERIDGE

TEME

RIVER

GREAT WESTERN, BROMYARD AND LEOMINSTER BRANCH

Malvern Link Gas Works Siding 162ᴹ62ᶜ

NEWLAND

GREAT WESTERN

1ᴹ65ᶜ

2ᴹ25ᶜ

30ᶜ

2ᴹ27ᶜ

WORCESTER AND MALVERN

BRANSFORD

LEIGH COURT

LEIGH SINTON

HEREFORD

From Leominster (WORCESTER, BROMYARD AND LEOMINSTER)

BROADWAS

COUNTY BOUNDARY

WORCESTER.

— WORCESTER —

WORCESTER TUNNEL 230 YARDS 156ᴹ26ᶜ

Junction of Joint Station Lines North 156ᴹ26ᶜ

G.W. Goods Lines Junction 156ᴹ31ᶜ

TUNNEL JUNCTION 156ᴹ28ᶜ

Tunnel Junction S.B. 156ᴹ33ᶜ

SHRUB HILL JUNCTION

Shrub Hill Junction S.B. 156ᴹ53ᶜ

Shrub Hill Junction 156ᴹ56ᶜ

G.W. GOODS STATION

SHRUB HILL PASSENGER STATION 156ᴹ62ᶜ (G.W. AND M. JOINT)

Shrub Hill Station S.B. 156ᴹ68ᶜ

Midland Goods Yard Junction North 157ᴹ5ᶜ

MIDLAND GOODS STATION 157ᴹ9ᶜ

G.W. Goods Lines Junction 157ᴹ11ᶜ

Wyld's Lane Junction S.B. 157ᴹ14ᶜ

WYLD'S LANE JUNCTION

Midland Goods Yard Junction South 157ᴹ19ᶜ

Junction of Joint Station Lines South 157ᴹ24ᶜ

To GLOUCESTER

M.R.

GOODS

20ᶜ

30ᶜ

32ᶜ

28ᶜ

3ᶜ

5ᶜ

7ᶜ

5ᶜ

5ᶜ

9ᶜ

17ᶜ

LINES

MIDLAND ENGINE SHED

To Birmingham

G.W.R.

RAINBOW HILL JUNCTION 156ᴹ56ᶜ

G.W.R.

Quay Branch Junction 157ᴹ10ᶜ

FOREGATE STREET 157ᴹ6ᶜ

GAS WORKS

FLOUR MILL

VULCAN IRON WORKS

VINEGAR WORKS

WORCESTER CANAL

Cross

Cathedral

Winchester Junction

G.W.R.

RIVER SEVERN

HENWICK 157ᴹ60ᶜ

ST. JOHN'S

Q.L.

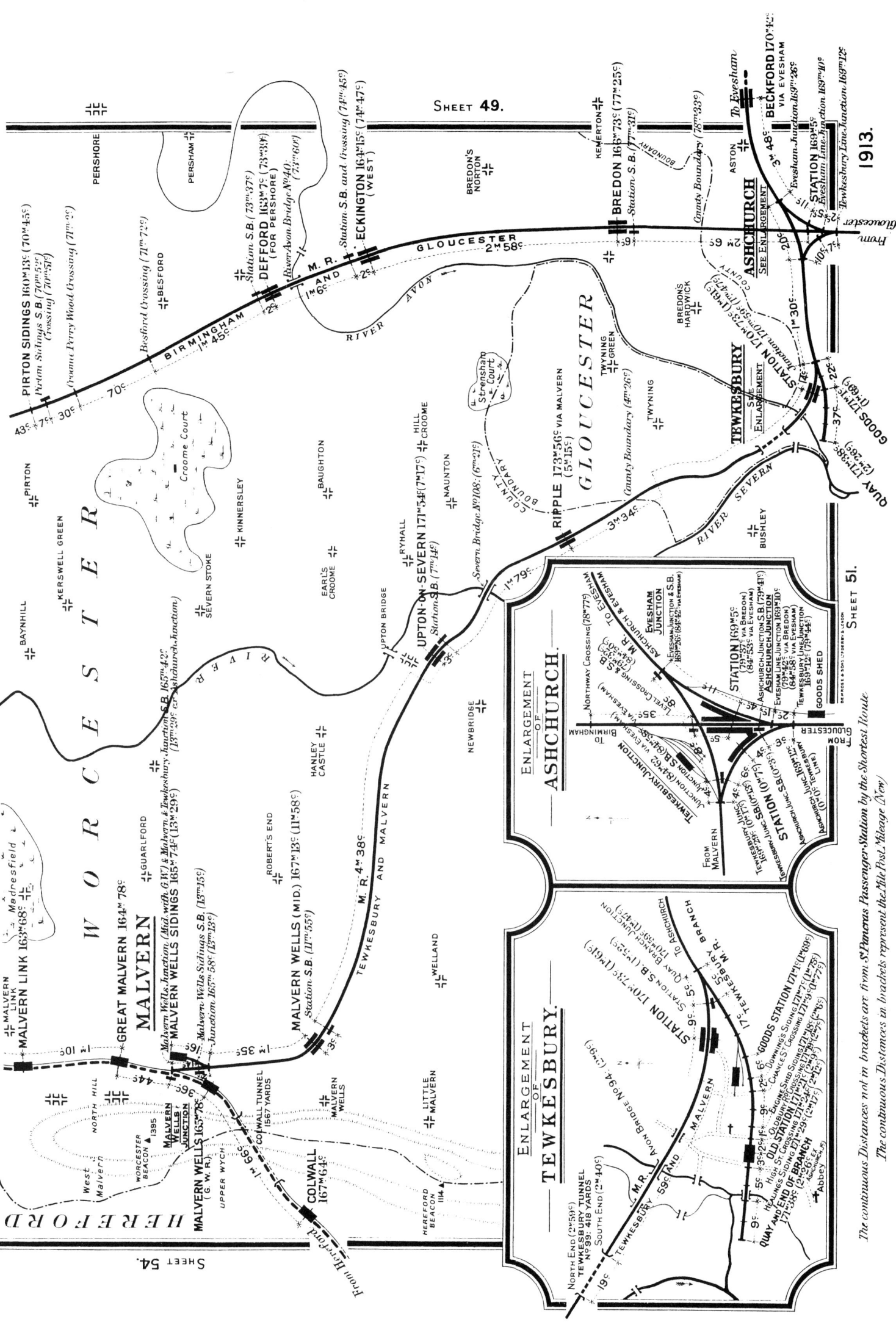

1913.

PERSHORE

PERSHAM

PIRTON SIDINGS 160M 13c (70M 45c)

Pirton Sidings S.B. (70M 52c)

Crossing (70M 51c)

(From Perry Wood Crossing (71M 0c))

Besford Crossing (71M 72c)

BESFORD

Station S.B. (73M 37c)

DEFFORD 163M 7c (73M 33c)

(FOR PERSHORE)

River Avon Bridge No 40 (73M 60c)

Station S.B. and Crossing (74M 45c)

ECKINGTON 164M 15c (74M 47c) (WEST)

BIRMINGHAM AND GLOUCESTER

M.R.

BREDON'S NORTON

KEMERTON

BREDON 166M 73c (77M 25c)

Station S.B. (77M 31c)

RIVER AVON

To Evesham

BECKFORD 170M 42c

3M 48c

via Evesham

Evesham Junction 169M 26c

Evesham Line Junction 169M 41c

Tewkesbury Line Junction 169M 12c

STATION 169M 5c

ASTON

ASHCHURCH
SEE ENLARGEMENT

From Gloucester

County Boundary

BREDONS HARDWICK

TWYNING GREEN

TWYNING

STRENSHAM COURT

County Boundary (4M 26c)

County Boundary

TEWKESBURY
SEE ENLARGEMENT

GOODS 171M (2M 58c)

QUAY 171M 38c (2M 56c)

RIVER SEVERN

BUSHLEY

PIRTON

BAYNHILL

KERSWELL GREEN

SEVERN STOKE

Croome Court

KINNERSLEY

BAUGHTON

EARLS CROOME

HILL CROOME

RYHALL

RIPPLE 173M 50c via Malvern (5M 15c)

GLOUCESTER

Severn Bridge No 108. (6M 21c)

NAUNTON

UPTON-ON-SEVERN 171M 54c (7M 17c)

Station S.B. (7M 14c)

WORCESTER

Madresfield

Malvern Link

MALVERN LINK 163M 68c

GREAT MALVERN 164M 78c

MALVERN

West Malvern

WORCESTER BEACON ▲1395

NORTH HILL

GUARLFORD

Malvern Wells Junction (Mid. with G.W.) & Malvern & Tewkesbury Junction S.B. 165M 42c
(13M 29c) (Ashchurch Junction)

MALVERN WELLS SIDINGS 165M 74c (13M 29c)

Malvern Wells Sidings S.B. (13M 15c)

Malvern 165M 58c Junction 165M 43c

MALVERN WELLS 165M 78c (G.W.R.)

MALVERN WELLS JUNCTION

Colwall Tunnel 1567 YARDS

UPPER WYCH

HEREFORD BEACON ▲1114

LITTLE MALVERN

MALVERN WELLS

COLWALL 167M 64c

From Hereford

MALVERN WELLS (MID.) 167M 13c (11M 58c)

Station S.B. (11M 55c)

ROBERT'S END

HANLEY CASTLE

UPTON BRIDGE

NEWBRIDGE

WELLAND

M.R. 4M 38c

TEWKESBURY AND MALVERN

W O R C E S T E R

H E R E F O R D

R I V E R

Sheet 54.

ENLARGEMENT OF ASHCHURCH.

Northway Crossing (78M 79c)

TO EVESHAM

Evesham Junction & S.B. 169M 26c
(84M 42c via Evesham)

STATION 169M 5c

Ashchurch Junction S.B. (84M 53c via Evesham)

ASHCHURCH JUNCTION

Evesham Line Junction (84M 58c via Evesham)

Tewkesbury Line Junction 169M 12c (79M 44c)

GOODS SHED

Level Crossing (84M 35c via Evesham)

To Birmingham

M.R.

FROM GLOUCESTER

ASHCHURCH JUNCTION

TEWKESBURY JUNCTION 169M 12c (0M 0c via Tewkesbury line)

Tewkesbury Junc. S.B. (0M 7c)

STATION S.B. (0M 3c)

Ashchurch Junc. 169M 12c (0M 0c Tewkesbury Line)

To Ashchurch

FROM MALVERN

To Birmingham via Evesham

ENLARGEMENT OF TEWKESBURY.

North End (2M 59c)

Tewkesbury Tunnel 418 YARDS

South End (2M 40c)

M.R. TEWKESBURY AND MALVERN

STATION 170M 73c (1M 61c)

Quay Branch S.B. (1M 55c)

QUAY BRANCH JUNCTION 170M 59c (1M 47c)

TEWKESBURY BRANCH

Avon Bridge No 94. (2M 9c)

Downing's Siding (1M 69c)

Engine Shed Siding (1M 78c)

Chance's Crossing (1M 75c)

GOODS STATION 171M 40c (1M 78c)

OLD STATION 171M 29c (1M 75c)

High St Crossing 171M 18c

QUAY AND END OF BRANCH 171M 38c (2M 26c)

HEADINGS SIDING 171M 9c (2M 5c)

Abbey

The continuous Distances not in brackets are from St Pancras Passenger Station by the Shortest Route.

The continuous Distances in brackets represent the Mile Post Mileage (New).

Sheet 51.

Oxenton Hill .734

To Birmingham

GOTHERINGTON

BISHOPS CLEEVE

(CHELTENHAM & DISTRICT

WESTERN HONEYBOURNE)

LIGHT RAILWAY

AND

GREAT WESTERN

(CHELTENHAM

From Birmingham

ASHCHURCH

Tewkesbury Line Junction 169ᵐ42ᶜ (79ᵐ44ᶜ)

Home Down Crossing 169ᵐ56ᶜ (80ᵐ8ᶜ)

Fiddington Crossing 170ᵐ7ᶜ (80ᵐ39ᶜ)

Tredington (Crossing) 171ᵐ11ᶜ (81ᵐ43ᶜ)

44ᶜ   31ᶜ   1ᵐ4ᶜ

1ᵐ31ᶜ   1ᵐ31ᶜ

BIRMINGHAM   AND   GLOUCESTER

1ᵐ25ᶜ   3ᶜ   M. R.

CLEEVE 172ᵐ42ᶜ (82ᵐ74ᶜ)

Station S.B. 172ᵐ47ᶜ (82ᵐ79ᶜ)

Swindon Crossing 173ᵐ72ᶜ (84ᵐ24ᶜ)

Morris Hill Crossing 174ᵐ5ᶜ (85ᵐ37ᶜ)

599   689   633

SWINDON

CHELTENHAM GOODS 175ᵐ39ᶜ (85ᵐ71ᶜ)

HIGH STREET HALT

ST JAMES SQUARE

CHELTENHAM (PASSENGER) 176ᵐ24ᶜ (86ᵐ56ᶜ)

—SEE— ENLARGEMENT

LANSDOWN ROAD   MALVERN ROAD

LANSDOWN JUNCTION

Honeybourne Line Junction 176ᵐ33ᶜ (86ᵐ71ᶜ)

Chipping Norton Line Junction 176ᵐ40ᶜ (86ᵐ72ᶜ)

Gloucester Loop Junction

PRESTBURY

SOUTHAM

CHELTENHAM SOUTH AND LECKHAMPTON

CHARLTON KINGS

CHARLTON KINGS

GREAT   BANBURY AND CHELTENHAM

LECKHAMPTON

To Chipping Norton and Cirencester

500

STOKE ORCHARD

WALTON CARDIFF

TREDINGTON

ELMSTON HARDWICKE

UCKINGTON

BODDINGTON

STAVERTON

GOLDEN VALLEY

UP HATHERLEY

BADGEWORTH

GREAT SHURDINGTON

CHURCHDOWN (JOINT STATION) 179ᵐ36ᶜ (89ᵐ68ᶜ)

Station S.B. 179ᵐ34ᶜ (89ᵐ66ᶜ)

Hatherley Junction 177ᵐ15ᶜ (87ᵐ47ᶜ)

G.W. MAINTENANCE TO LANSDOWN JUNCTION

G.W. AND MID MAINTENANCE BOARD 179ᵐ51ᶜ (90ᵐ3ᶜ)

MIDLAND MAINTENANCE FROM GLOUCESTER

CHURCHDOWN

Churchdown Hill 400

DEERHURST WALTON

DEERHURST

RIVER SEVERN

Forthampton Court

CHACELEY

TEWKESBURY

ABBEY

COOMBE HILL

BARROW

LEIGH

NORTON

DOWN HATHERLEY

STAVERTON BRIDGE

Tramway Junction 182ᵐ76ᶜ (93ᵐ8ᶜ)

G.W. STATION   G.W. MIDLAND GOODS 182ᵐ76ᶜ

Mid and G.W. Junction 182ᵐ66ᶜ (93ᵐ18ᶜ)

GREAT WESTERN

RIVER SEVERN

MAISEMORE

SANDHURST

WALLSWORTH

LONGFORD

TWIGWORTH

BISHOPS NORTON

ASHLEWORTH

HARTPURY

From Ledbury

LASSINGTON

HIGHNAM

G.W. & MID LINE

G.W.R.

GLOUCESTER

Hatherley Junction S.B. 177ᵐ48ᶜ (87ᵐ47ᶜ)

Lansdown Junction Main S.B. 176ᵐ41ᶜ (86ᵐ73ᶜ)

G L O U C E S T E R

ENLARGEMENT —OF— CHELTENHAM.

LANSDOWN JUNCTION

To Birmingham

TEWKESBURY ROAD COAL WHARF 175ᵐ23ᶜ (85ᵐ55ᶜ)

HIGH STREET HALT (G.W.)

Corporation Siding Junction 175ᵐ34ᶜ (85ᵐ66ᶜ)

Mland S.W. Junction Coys Sidings

High Street S.B. 175ᵐ34ᶜ (85ᵐ68ᶜ)

Gas Works

CHELTENHAM GOODS 175ᵐ39ᶜ (85ᵐ71ᶜ)

Junction for Gas Works 175ᵐ42ᶜ (85ᵐ74ᶜ)

Alston Junction S.(B. and Crossing 175ᵐ69ᶜ (86ᵐ21ᶜ)

ALSTON COAL WHARF

Alston Down Line Junction 175ᵐ70ᶜ (86ᵐ22ᶜ)

Junction of Martyns Siding 175ᵐ74ᶜ (86ᵐ26ᶜ)

Alston Coal Wharf Junction 176ᵐ3ᶜ (86ᵐ35ᶜ)

ST JAMES'S SQUARE (G.W. STATION)

G.W.R. Mid M. & S.W. Junction Cᵒˢ

Down Goods Line Junction 176ᵐ18ᶜ (86ᵐ50ᶜ)

G.W.R. MALVERN ROAD STATION (G.W.)

MALVERN ROAD JUNCTION

Station S.B. 176ᵐ21ᶜ (86ᵐ53ᶜ)

LANSDOWN (PASSENGER) 176ᵐ24ᶜ (86ᵐ56ᶜ)

Honeybourne Line Junction 176ᵐ40ᶜ (86ᵐ72ᶜ)

End of Midland Maintenance 176ᵐ36ᶜ (86ᵐ68ᶜ)

Chipping Norton Line Junction 176ᵐ40ᶜ (86ᵐ72ᶜ)

Lansdown Junction Main. S.B. 176ᵐ41ᶜ (86ᵐ73ᶜ)

Joint Sidings Mid. & M. & S.W. Junction

Gloucester Loop Junction

G.W.R.   To Chipping Norton & Cirencester

G.W.R.   FROM GLOUCESTER

11ᶜ   3ᶜ   3ᶜ   32ᶜ   15ᶜ   12ᶜ   33ᶜ   15ᶜ   3ᶜ

GLOUCESTER.

— ENLARGEMENT — OF — GLOUCESTER.

1911.

SHEET 52.

THOS. KELL & SON, LONDON.

GLOUCESTER
— SEE —
— ENLARGEMENT —

PASSENGER STATION 182ᵐ60ᶜ(93ᵐ12ᶜ)
Barton Street Junction (Docks Branch) 182ᵐ74ᶜ(93ᵐ3ᶜ)
Engine Shed Junction 182ᵐ71ᶜ(92ᵐ23ᶜ)
Tuffley Junction 184ᵐ41ᶜ(97ᵐ70ᶜ)

Engine Shed Junction(GWR)181ᵐ51ᶜ(92ᵐ28ᶜ)
Goods Junction S.B.Bar Entry Junction 181ᵐ76ᶜ(92ᵐ28ᶜ)
Engine Shed Junction(GWR)181ᵐ76ᶜ(92ᵐ28ᶜ)
Down Goods Line Junction 181ᵐ78ᶜ(92ᵐ30ᶜ)
Engine Shed Sidings S.B.181ᵐ78ᶜ(92ᵐ30ᶜ)
MIDLAND ENGINE SHEDS
Barnwood Junction(GW)182ᵐ36ᶜ(92ᵐ68ᶜ)
BARNWOOD 182ᵐ36ᶜ(92ᵐ68ᶜ)
Barnwood Junction & S.B.182ᵐ18ᶜ(92ᵐ50ᶜ)
Barnwood Sidings
Tramway Junction(GW)182ᵐ38ᶜ
Tramway Junction S.B.& Crossing 182ᵐ33ᶜ
Tramway Junction S.B.& Crossing
End of Mid.MAINTENANCE
Goods.Junc.S.Bar End & Junction 182ᵐ40ᶜ(92ᵐ72ᶜ)
Goods Station S.B.182ᵐ45ᶜ(92ᵐ77ᶜ)
Goods Junc.S.Bar End & Junction
PASSENGER STATION 182ᵐ60ᶜ(93ᵐ12ᶜ)
Passenger Station (Phillips)182ᵐ45ᶜ(92ᵐ77ᶜ)
Barton Street Junction(Goods Lines)182ᵐ60ᶜ
Barton Street Junction(Docks Branch)182ᵐ74ᶜ(93ᵐ3ᶜ)
Chequers Road Junction 182ᵐ74ᶜ(93ᵐ46ᶜ)AND JUNCTION
Pembroke Street Crossing S.B.182ᵐ37ᶜ(93ᵐ8ᶜ)
Pembroke Street Crossing
California Crossing & S.B.183ᵐ4ᶜ(93ᵐ46ᶜ)
Bowles's Crossing 183ᵐ23ᶜ(93ᵐ50ᶜ)
Painswick Rᵈ Crossing 183ᵐ40ᶜ(93ᵐ72ᶜ)
Painswick Rᵈ Crossing S.B.183ᵐ41ᶜ(93ᵐ73ᶜ)

PASSENGER STATION

G.W.STATION

Cathedral

The Cross

OVER JUNCTION
DOCK JUNCTION
VICTORIA DOCK
EAST CHANNEL
GREAT WESTERN
RIVER SEVERN
SOUTH GREAT WESTERN LINE
GREAT WESTERN & SOUTH WALES LINE
FROM CARDIFF

GREAT WESTERN
MIDLAND

HIGH ORCHARD YARD
TIMBER YARDS

STONEHOUSE JUNCTION LINE
Double Line Junc.185ᵐ14ᶜ(95ᵐ46ᶜ)
Canal Swing Bridge Nº4.185ᵐ37ᶜ(95ᵐ69ᶜ)
Canal Bridge S.B.185ᵐ36ᶜ(95ᵐ68ᶜ)
Collett's Siding 185ᵐ28ᶜ(95ᵐ55ᶜ)
TG⁷⁹ Hempsted Wharf Junction 185ᵐ22ᶜ(95ᵐ54ᶜ)

HEMPSTED WHARF 185ᵐ34ᶜ(95ᵐ66ᶜ)
TUFFLEY, OR GLOUCESTER NEW DOCKS BRANCH
GLOUCESTER
Gas Works

Tuffley Junction S.B.184ᵐ40ᶜ(94ᵐ72ᶜ)
Tuffley Branch Junction 184ᵐ41ᶜ(94ᵐ73ᶜ)AND TUFFLEY WHARF

UNION AND G.W.R.
CHELTENHAM G.W.R.AND
FROM SWINDON
FROM BRISTOL

BERKELEY SHIP CANAL

The continuous Distances not in brackets are
from St. Pancras Passenger Station, by the shortest Route.
The continuous Distances in brackets represent the Mile Post Mileage (New) and are from London Rd. Junction Derby via Whitacre.

To Birmingham
To Swindon

GLOUCESTER SHIP CANAL AND BERKELEY

RIVER SEVERN (SOUTH)

Leckhampton Hill 806
Ullenwood
800
800
800

COBERLEY

BENTHAM

BROCKWORTH

HUCCLECOTE
BARNWOOD
Bowdon Park
UPTON LEONARDS
MATSON
651 Robin's Wood Hill
WHADDON
TUFFLEY

PAINSWICK
PITCHCOMBE
HARESCOMBE
BROOKTHORPE

STROUD
PASSENGER 194ᵐ62ᶜ(105ᵐ14ᶜ)
GOODS 195ᵐ2ᶜ(105ᵐ54ᶜ)
To Swindon
Wimbridge Crossing Halt
RODBOROUGH
Downfield Crossing Halt 194ᵐ45ᶜ(105ᵐ25ᶜ)
DUDBRIDGE 193ᵐ14ᶜ(104ᵐ46ᶜ)
DUDBRIDGE JUNCTION 193ᵐ18ᶜ(104ᵐ5ᶜ)
To Nailsworth
STONEHOUSE AND NAILSWORTH
STROUDWATER CANAL

STANDISH JUNCTION
HARESFIELD 188ᵐ27ᶜ(98ᵐ59ᶜ)
Haresfield Station S.B.and Crossing 188ᵐ46ᶜ(98ᵐ25ᶜ)
Naas Crossing and S.B.187ᵐ49ᶜ(97ᵐ97ᶜ)
End of M.R.188ᵐ62ᶜ(100ᵐ14ᶜ)
M.R.AND G.W.R.(STONEHOUSE JUNCTION LINE)
GLOUCESTER AND BRISTOL (STONEHOUSE AND CHELTENHAM)
WESTERN GREAT

STONEHOUSE G.W.R.
RYEFORD 192ᵐ9ᶜ(103ᵐ2ᶜ)(95ᵐ)
Ebley Crossing Halt
Stonehouse Junction 191ᵐ27ᶜ(101ᵐ59ᶜ)
Stonehouse Junction S.B.191ᵐ15ᶜ(101ᵐ47ᶜ)
Nupend Junction 191ᵐ13ᶜ(101ᵐ75ᶜ)(102ᵐ7ᶜ)
Upend Junction 190ᵐ75ᶜ(101ᵐ27ᶜ)
Landswick
STANDISH
STANDISH JUNCTION S.B.
Standish Junction S.B.188ᵐ58ᶜ(100ᵐ10ᶜ)
Standish Junction 188ᵐ54ᶜ(100ᵐ6ᶜ)
VIADUCT Nº85 (102ᵐ9ᶜ)

HARDWICKE
QUEDGELEY
HEMPSTED
MEMPSTED

From Bristol

MIDLAND RAILWAY DISTANCE DIAGRAM. SCALE 1½ INCHES TO 1 MILE.
GREAT WESTERN AND MIDLAND.
SEVERN AND WYE JOINT LINES.

BOOK No. 76

To Gloucester

GREAT WESTERN — From Hereford & Ross — To Gloucester

FLAXLEY

ABINGHALL

LITTLE DEAN

RIVER SEVERN

NEWNHAM

Dock Junction

RUDDLE ROAD HALT

BULLO PILL GOODS

BULLO PILL DOCK

Ferry

BULLO CROSS HALT

WESTERN BRANCH

UPPER SOUDLEY HALT

SOUDLEY FURNACES

GREAT FOREST OF DEAN

WESTERN

RUARDEAN

SITE OF OLD BISHOPSWOOD TRAMWAY

DRYBROOK HALT

DRYBROOK

Nailbridge Tramway

STEAM MILLS CROSSING HALT

WHIMSEY HALT

Cinderford Junction (G.W.R.) 18ᵐ·30ᶜ and S.B.
Cinderford Junction
Bilson South Junction with G.W. 18ᵐ·14ᶜ
Station S.B. 18ᵐ·52ᶜ
CINDERFORD
CINDERFORD 18ᵐ·60ᶜ

BILSON HALT
BILSON GOODS
CRUMP MEADOW COLLIERY

RUSPIDGE GOODS
Junction for Colliery (mean) 16ᵐ·40ᶜ
RUSPIDGE

LIGHTMOOR COLLIERY
STAPLE EDGE HALT
End of Joint Line 15ᵐ·39ᶜ

GREAT FOREST OF DEAN

MINERAL LOOP 17ᵐ·14ᶜ

DRYBROOK ROAD HALT

CHURCHWAY BRANCH

TRAFALGAR COLLIERY

BRIERLEY

Brierley Stone Siding 18ᵐ·4ᶜ

ARTHUR & EDWARD COLLIERY

Serridge Junction
Serridge Junction S.B. 16ᵐ·30ᶜ
Crown Siding 16ᵐ·25ᶜ

Junction 17ᵐ·1ᶜ

FOXES BRIDGE COLLIERY

FOREST OF DEAN

Speech House

Station Loop North 14ᵐ·72ᶜ
Wimberry Branch Junction 14ᵐ·70ᶜ
Station S.B. and Crossing 14ᵐ·69ᶜ
SPEECH HOUSE ROAD 14ᵐ·67ᶜ
Howlerslade Siding 14ᵐ·54ᶜ
Loop Junction 14ᵐ·51ᶜ

NEW FANCY COLLIERY
New Fancy Colliery Junction 14ᵐ·67ᶜ
Bicslade Siding 15ᵐ·62ᶜ

COLEFORD BRANCH JUNCTION
Coleford Branch Junction 13ᵐ·12ᶜ
Brick Pit Sidings Junction 13ᵐ·45ᶜ
Speech Log Junction 12ᵐ·71ᶜ
Coleford Branch Junction 13ᵐ·48ᶜ
6ᵗʰ Division of Maintenance 13ᵐ·65ᶜ

HOWBEACH COLLIERY

WELSH BICKNOR
Bickmor Public Siding 20ᵐ·41ᶜ
Courtfield
LYDBROOK VIADUCT : 19ᵐ·67ᶜ & 19ᵐ·76ᶜ
LYDBROOK 20ᵐ·10ᶜ
LYDBROOK JUNCTION STA. 20ᵐ·61ᶜ
Loop Junction 20ᵐ·51ᶜ
Lydbrook Junction S.B. 20ᵐ·40ᶜ
Junction of S. & W. Joint Line with G.W.R. 20ᵐ·69ᶜ

UPPER LYDBROOK 18ᵐ·78ᶜ
Loop North 19ᵐ·35ᶜ
Loop South 18ᵐ·72ᶜ — S.B. & Crossing 18ᵐ·75ᶜ
TUNNEL 19ᵐ·8ᶜ and 19ᵐ·9ᶜ

ENGLISH BICKNOR

CHRISTCHURCH

MIERY STOCK TUNNEL
North End 17ᵐ·72ᶜ
South End 17ᵐ·61ᶜ
End of Joint Line 17ᵐ·57ᶜ
Miery Stock Siding Junction 17ᵐ·38ᶜ
Speculation Siding 17ᵐ·3ᶜ
SITE OF SPECULATION CURVE

Whitegates Junction (Closed)

CANNOP COLLIERY
Cannop Ponds
BIXHEAD QUARRY

WIMBERRY TRAMWAY
HOWLERSLADE TRAMWAY
BICSLADE TRAMWAY

Howlershill Quarry 15ᵐ·58ᶜ
United Stone Farms

Spion Kop Quarry
United Stone Farms

Point Quarry or Dark Hill Siding

COLEFORD
S. AND W. STATION 16ᵐ·49ᶜ
(FOR STAUNTON)
Junction 16ᵐ·34ᶜ

MILKWALL (FOR CLEARWELL)
15ᵐ·47ᶜ

G.W. STATION
Junction with G.W.R. 16ᵐ·37ᶜ

Sling Branch Junction 15ᵐ·50ᶜ
Easter Iron Ore Mines
Iron Ore Dock
Sling Sidings 16ᵐ·op.
Watkin & Soils Iron Ore Mines

To Ross
RIVER WYE
From Monmouth
End of Joint Line 19ᵐ·68ᶜ
S. AND W. SIDINGS
MONMOUTH

WEST DEAN
MAIN LINE

SHEET 52.

1917.

BERKELEY ROAD JUNCTION

M.R.

From Bristol

Berkeley Road South Junction

Berkeley Loop 1 mile

Berkeley Loop Junction

Berkeley Loop

Berkeley

Castle

Little Avon River

Berkeley Pill

Bull Rock

Lights

NOTE:- 3 Miles additional allowed for the SEVERN BRIDGE by Act of Parliament of 1872. ACTUAL LENGTH 55 CHAINS.

BERKELEY BRANCH 6⁷ᶜ

Sharpness S.B.

SHARPNESS
Dock Branch Junction (North) 4ᵐ·24ᶜ
Single Lane Junction 4ᵐ·22ᶜ
PASSENGER 4ᵐ·15ᶜ (AND CATTLE)
Goods Lines Junction North 4ᵐ·7ᶜ
OLDMINSTER SIDINGS
South Junction with Dock Lines 3ᵐ·74ᶜ
South Junction S.B. 3ᵐ·51ᶜ
Dock Branch Junction (South) 3ᵐ·44ᶜ
Oldminster Goods Lines Junction South 3ᵐ·43ᶜ

Canal Swing Bridge S.B. 4ᵐ·53ᶜ

GLOUCESTER

SHIP CANAL

BERKELEY CANAL

PURTON
HINTON

The Bridge

Waveridge Sand

Frampton Sands

WESTERN

Severn Bridge Tunnel

DOCKS & COAL 5⁷ᶜ

Light

SEVERN

Purton Sand

Sharpness

SEVERN BRIDGE STATION 5ᵐ·40ᶜ
Loop 5ᵐ·34ᶜ and 5ᵐ·50ᶜ S.B. 5ᵐ·42ᶜ
North End 5ᵐ·6ᶜ

PURTON
Purton S.B. 5ᵐ·11ᶜ

GREAT

WESTERN

SOUTH WALES LINE

LYDNEY
SEE ENLARGEMENT
LYDNEY HARBOUR
UPPER DOCK 9ᵐ·16ᶜ
LOWER DOCK 9ᵐ·72ᶜ

Lydney Sand

RIVER SEVERN

Guscar Sand

SEVERN BRIDGE TUNNEL No.19. 506 YDS.
South End 6ᵐ·5ᶜ

AWRE
Awre Junction

WESTERN RAILWAY

OF DEAN CENTRAL

BLAKENEY GOODS
BLAKENEY

End of Midland Maintenance on Loop Line 11ᵐ·0ᶜ

PARKEND
PASSENGER 12ᵐ·25ᶜ
Junction 12ᵐ·18ᶜ

North End 12ᵐ·70ᶜ
MOSELEY GREEN TUNNEL
SOUTH END 12ᵐ·47ᶜ

PARK END ROYAL COLLIERY

YORKLEY

PILLOWELL
Pillowell Level Crossing 11ᵐ·43ᶜ

WHITECROFT 11ᵐ·21ᶜ
Station S.B. and Crossing 11ᵐ·24ᶜ
VIADUCT 11ᵐ·29ᶜ

TUFTS JUNCTION
Loop Line Junction 10ᵐ·60ᶜ
Tufts Junction S.B. 10ᵐ·56ᶜ
Oakwood Branch Junction 10ᵐ·54ᶜ
Double Line Junction 10ᵐ·49ᶜ

End of Oakwood Branch 11ᵐ·45ᶜ
OAKWOOD BRANCH EXTENSION
PARK GUTTER COLLIERY 11ᵐ·42ᶜ
(PRINCESS ROYAL COLL⁽ COY⁾)

FLOUR MILL COLLIERY
(PRINCESS ROYAL COLL⁽ COY⁾)

EMPTY WAGON SIDINGS

TRAMWAY

OAKWOOD COLLIERY
NOT LAID

Chemical Coy's Siding 10ᵐ·63ᶜ

BREAM

Upper Forge Crossing 10ᵐ·2ᶜ

Middle Forge Crossing 9ᵐ·73ᶜ

Lower Forge Crossing 9ᵐ·52ᶜ

Cannop Brook or the Lyd

NORCHARD COLLIERY
Norchard Colliery Sidings 9ᵐ·52ᶜ

TOWN STATION 8ᵐ·78ᶜ

LYDNEY
SEE ENLARGEMENT

FLOUR MILL
CLEARWELL STONE FIRM and
Clearwell Stone Firm's Road S.B.
Futterill Branch Junction 13ᵐ·26ᶜ
The Futterill Siding Junction 13ᵐ·34ᶜ
Point Quarry Siding Junction 13ᵐ·0ᶜ

AWOOD GOODS 12ᵐ·44ᶜ

BRANCH

THE MOORS JUNCTION 8ᵐ·32ᶜ
LYDNEY JUNCTION STATION 8ᵐ·15ᶜ
(Junction Footbridge)

LYDNEY

LYDNEY HARBOUR

GLOUCESTER

Single Line Junction 9ᵐ·0ᶜ
TOWN STATION 8ᵐ·73ᶜ
Station S.B. & Crossing 8ᵐ·76ᶜ
3 Lines Junction 8ᵐ·70ᶜ
Arnold Perrett & Coy's Siding 8ᵐ·68ᶜ

From Lydbrook

LYDNEY TIN PLATE WORKS 8ᵐ·43ᶜ
Junction 8ᵐ·36ᶜ
LYDNEY COLOUR WORKS
Junction 8ᵐ·36ᶜ
Lydney Yard S.B. 8ᵐ·46ᶜ
LOCO SHED

X

To Berkeley Road
To Gloucester

WEST LOOP (MINERAL) JUNCTION 8ᵐ·55ᶜ
West Loop Junction S.B. (G.W) 7ᵐ·77ᶜ
DOUBLE LINE JUNCTION 7ᵐ·76ᶜ

WESTERN
SOUTH WALES LINE

OTTER'S POOL JUNCTION 7ᵐ·62ᶜ

THE MOORS (OR ENGINE SHED) JUNCTION 8ᵐ·32ᶜ
JUNCTION OF WEST LOOP TO G.W.R. 8ᵐ·22ᶜ
ENGINE SHED (INTERNAL) JUNCTION 8ᵐ·22ᶜ

JUNCTION STATION 8ᵐ·15ᶜ
Lydney Junction S.B. (G.W.) 7ᵐ·77ᶜ
East Loop Junction with G.W.R. 8ᵐ·1ᶜ

G.W. STATION

CANAL

Junction 8ᵐ·59ᶜ
Single Line Junction 8ᵐ·50ᶜ
G.W. LEVEL CROSSING AND
Upper Dock Branch Junction 8ᵐ·60ᶜ

LYDNEY WEST S.B.
SWING BRIDGE (No.2) 8ᵐ·62ᶜ

GREAT

From Cardiff

UPPER DOCK
LOWER DOCK 9ᵐ·72ᶜ
HARBOUR ENTRANCE

PIER

RIVER SEVERN

TIDAL BASIN
LOWER BASIN
SWING BRIDGE
UPPER BASIN

GOODS LINE

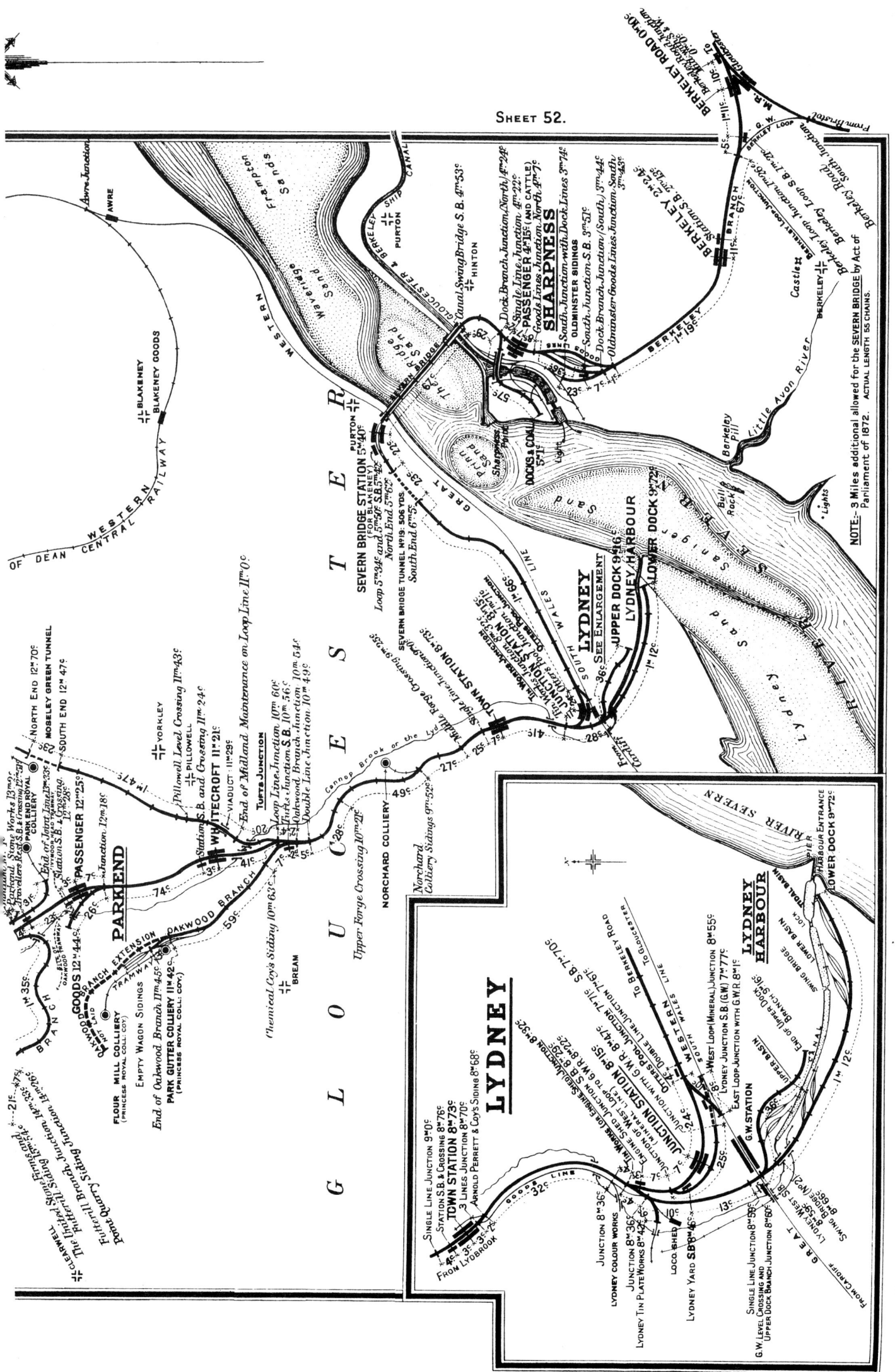

The continuous Distances are from BERKELEY ROAD JUNCTION and represent the Mile Post Mileage.

MIDLAND RAILWAY DISTANCE DIAGRAM. SCALE 1 INCH TO 1 MILE.

(STONEHOUSE TO YATE AND BRANCHES).

BOOK Nº 76

SHEET **52.** (Seventh Edition.)

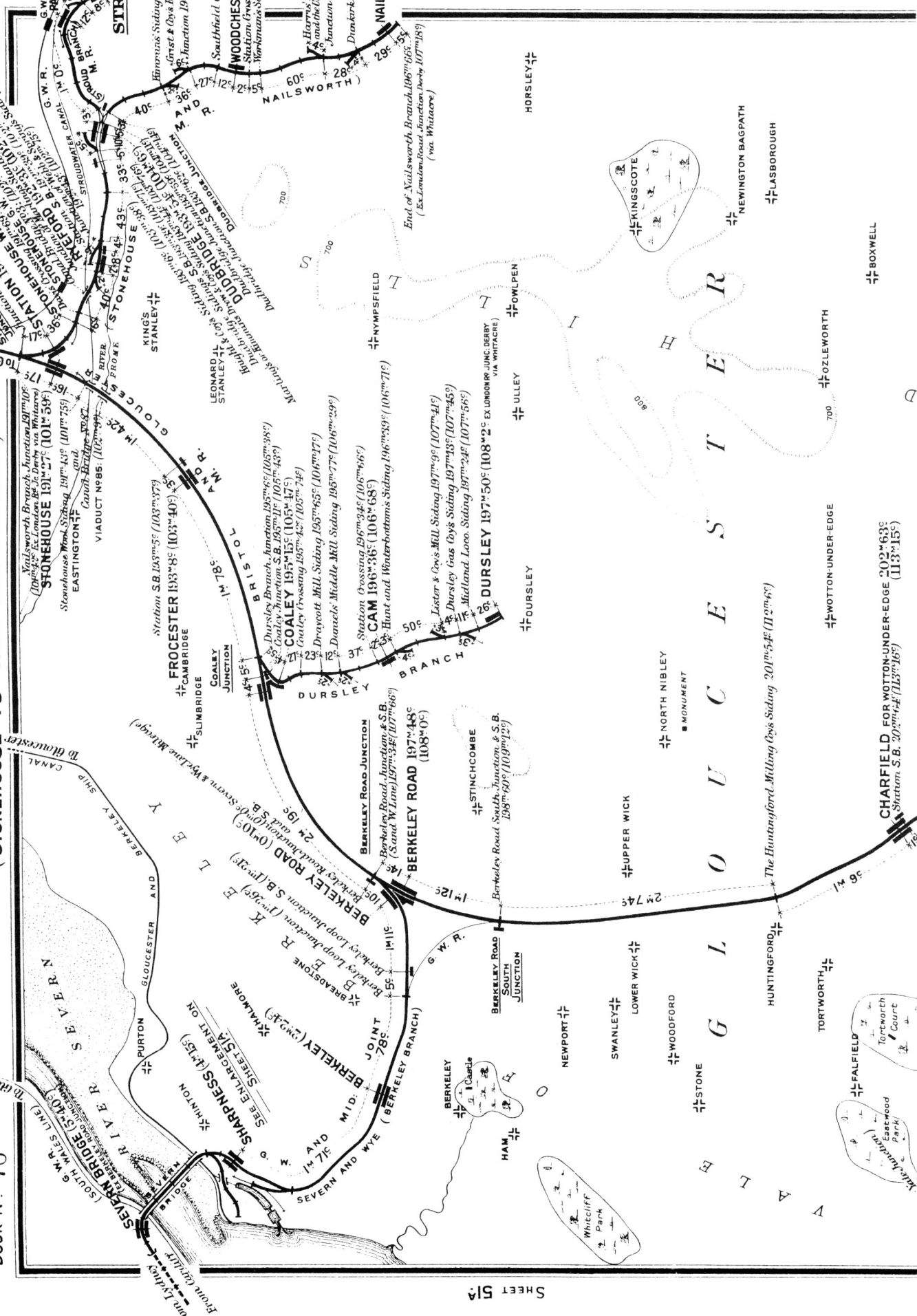

SHEET 51.

STROUD

GLOUCESTER

GLOUCESTERSHIRE

SEVERN RIVER

SHEET 51A

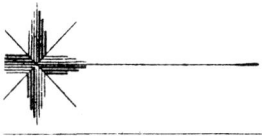

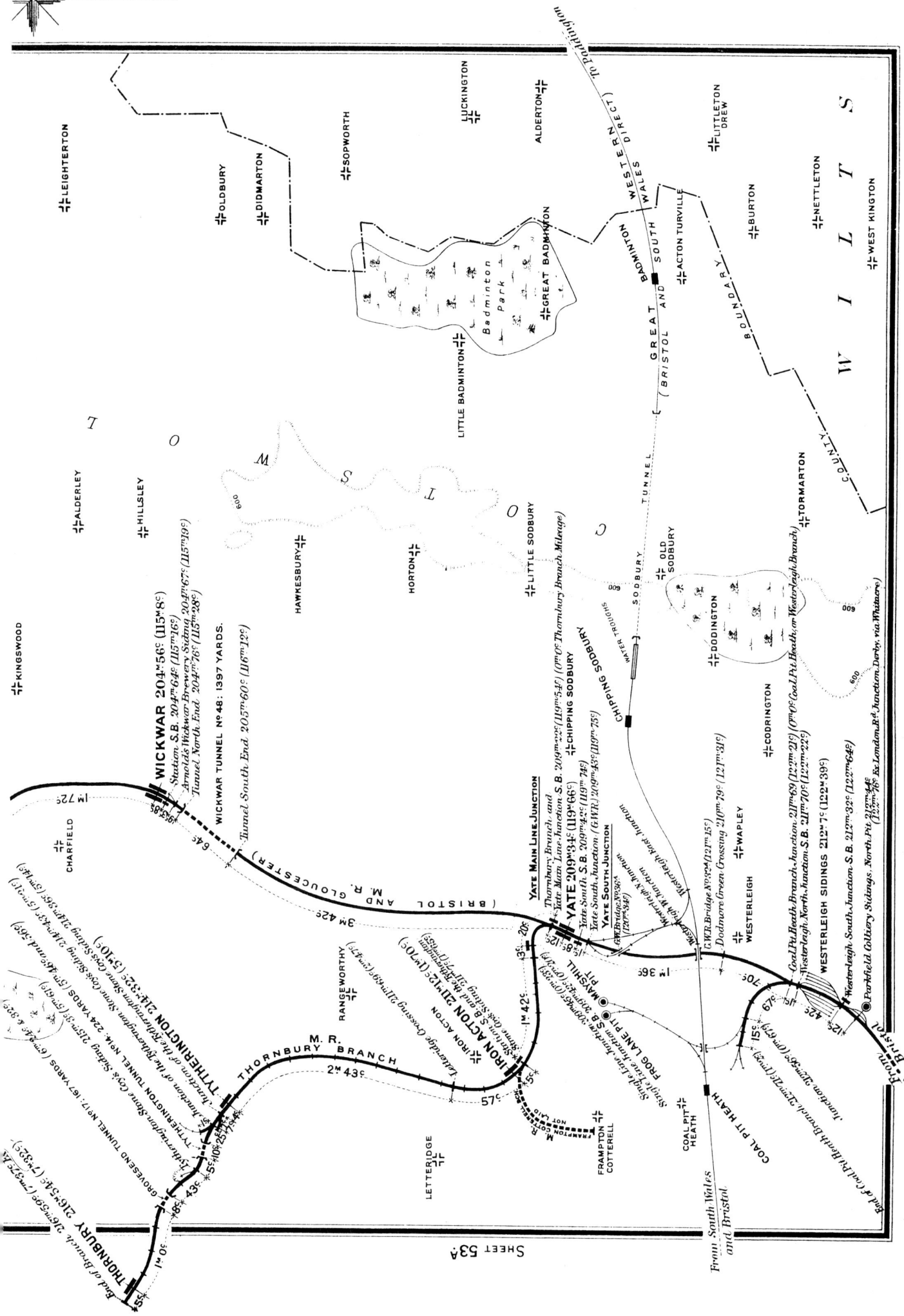

1913.

SHEET 53.

SHEET 53A.

Bemrose & Sons L.T.P Derby & London.

W I L T S

C O T S W O L D

Badminton Park

LEIGHTERTON
OLDBURY
DIDMARTON
SOPWORTH
LUCKINGTON
ALDERTON
GREAT BADMINTON
LITTLE BADMINTON
ACTON TURVILLE
LITTLETON DREW
BURTON
NETTLETON
WEST KINGTON
ALDERLEY
HILLSLEY
HAWKESBURY
HORTON
LITTLE SODBURY
CHIPPING SODBURY
OLD SODBURY
DODINGTON
CODRINGTON
WAPLEY
WESTERLEIGH
TORMARTON
KINGSWOOD
CHARFIELD
RANGEWORTHY
LETTERIDGE
FRAMPTON COTTERELL
COAL PIT HEATH

GREAT AND SOUTH WESTERN DIRECT (BRISTOL AND SOUTH WALES)
COUNTY BOUNDARY
To Paddington
SODBURY TUNNEL
WATER TROUGHS
From South Wales and Bristol

WICKWAR 204m 56c. (115m 8c.)
Station S.B. 204m 64c. (115m 16c.)
Arnold's Wickwar Brewery Siding 204m 67c. (115m 19c.)
Tunnel North End 204m 76c. (115m 28c.)
WICKWAR TUNNEL No 48: 1397 YARDS.
Tunnel South End 205m 60c. (116m 12c.)

(BRISTOL AND GLOUCESTER) M.R.
3m 42c
1m 72c
64c

YATE MAIN LINE JUNCTION
Thornbury Branch and
Yate Main Line Junction S.B. 209m 33c. (119m 66c.)
YATE 209m 34c. (119m 66c.)
Yate South S.B. 209m 42c. (119m 74c.)
Yate Junction (G.W.R.) 209m 43c. (119m 75c.)
YATE SOUTH JUNCTION
(0m 0c Thornbury Branch Mileage)

THORNBURY BRANCH M.R.
2m 43c
IRON ACTON 211m 12c. (121m 45c.)
Iron Acton S.B. and Siding 211m 12c. (121m 45c.)

THORNBURY 216m 59c. (126m 52c.)
End of Branch 216m 59c. (126m 52c.)
Tytherington Stone Co's Siding 214m 33c. (124m 26c.)
TYTHERINGTON
Tytherington Stone Co's Siding 214m 33c. (124m 26c.)
Junction of the Tytherington Stone Co's Siding 214m 32c. (124m 25c.)
TYTHERINGTON TUNNEL No 47: 187 yards.
GROVESEND TUNNEL 216m 54c. (126m 47c.)

MAYSHILL
FROG LANE PIT
1m 42c
Coal Pit Heath Branch Junction 211m 69c. (122m 2c.) (0m 0c Coal Pit Heath or Westerleigh Branch)
Westerleigh North Junction S.B. 211m 70c. (122m 3c.)
WESTERLEIGH SIDINGS 212m 7c. (122m 39c.)
Westerleigh South Junction S.B. 212m 32c. (122m 64c.)
Parkfield Colliery Sidings, North Pit 217m 44c.

G.W.R.Bridge No 364
Dodmore Green Crossing 210m 79c. (121m 31c.)

COAL PIT HEATH

The continuous Distances not in brackets are from St Pancras Passenger Station by the Shortest Route.
The continuous Distances in brackets represent the Mile Post Mileage (New)

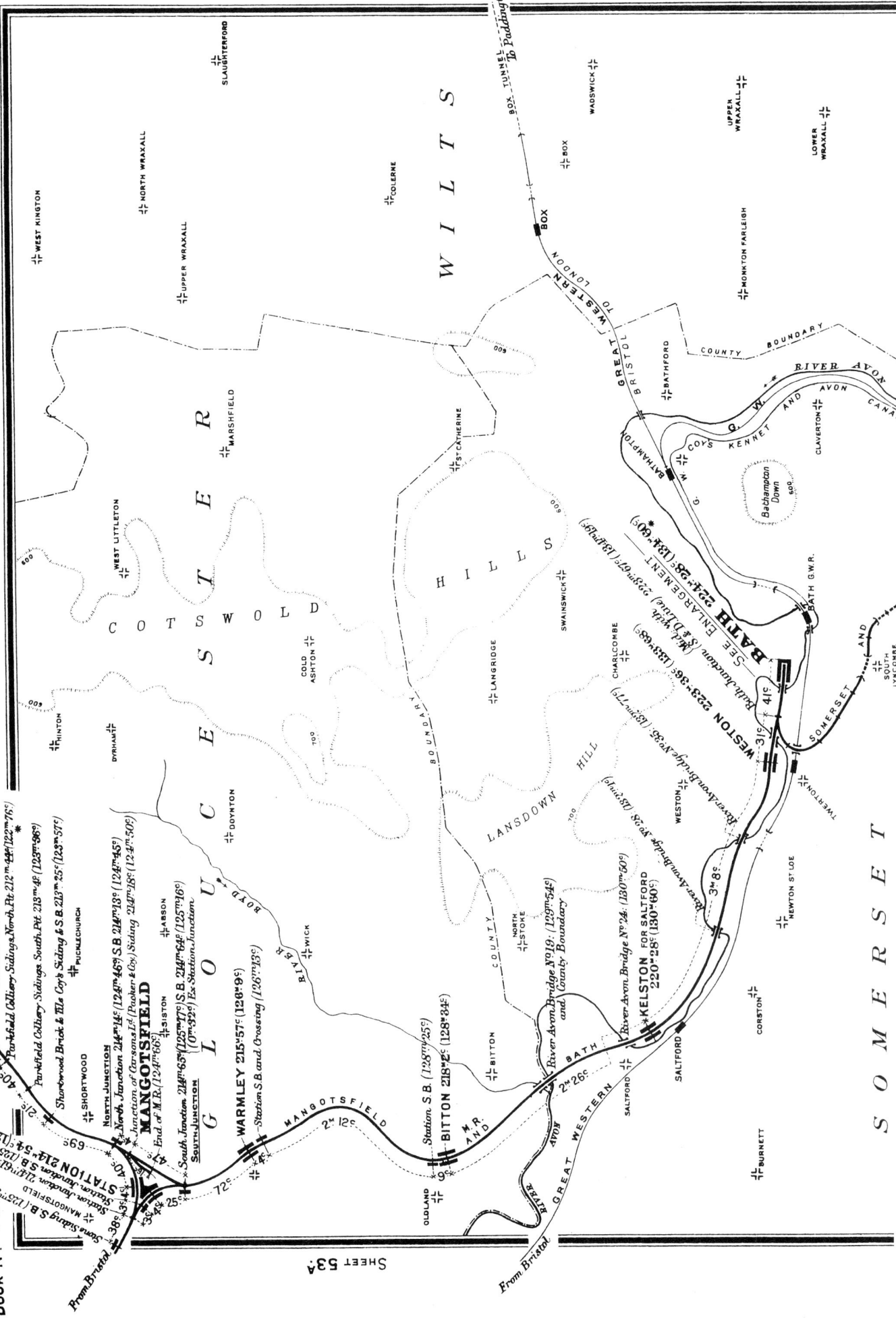

MIDLAND RAILWAY DISTANCE DIAGRAM. SCALE 1 INCH TO 1 MILE.
BATH DISTRICT.

SHEET 52.

BOOK No. 76.

W I L T S

G L O U C E S T E R

C O T S W O L D

H I L L S

LANSDOWN HILL

S O M E R S E T

SLAUGHTERFORD

NORTH WRAXALL

WEST KINGTON

UPPER WRAXALL

MARSHFIELD

WEST LITTLETON

HINTON

DYRHAM

DOYNTON

COLD ASHTON

ST CATHERINE

COLERNE

WADSWICK

BOX

UPPER WRAXALL

LOWER WRAXALL

MONKTON FARLEIGH

BATHFORD

COUNTY BOUNDARY

RIVER AVON

COYS KENNET AND AVON CANAL

CLAVERTON

BATHAMPTON

Bathampton Down

600

600

700

700

600

600

500

SWAINSWICK

LANGRIDGE

CHARLCOMBE

WESTON

NEWTON ST LOE

BATH G.W.R.

41c

31c

31c

TWERTON

SOUTH LYNCOMBE

BOX TUNNEL To Paddington

GREAT WESTERN TO LONDON

G.W.&B BRISTOL

BOX

BATHAMPTON

BATH 224.28c (134.60c)

WESTON 223.38c (133.88c)
Bath Junction (8ᵗʰ Line) 223.67c (134.09c)
SEE ENLARGEMENT

River Avon Bridge Nº35. 133⁄4pt 17c
River Avon Bridge Nº25. 132½m 9c
River Avon Bridge Nº19. 129m 54c and County Boundary
River Avon Bridge Nº24. 130m 50c

KELSTON FOR SALTFORD 220.28c (130.60c)

SALTFORD

Saltford

CORSTON

BURNETT

GREAT WESTERN

River Avon

OLDLAND

BITTON

M.R. AND

Station S.B. (128m 25c)
BITTON 218.25c (128m 34c)

3m 8c

2m 26c

2m 12c

9c

MANGOTSFIELD

RIVER BOYD

RIVER BRISLWICK

Station S.B. and Crossing (126m 13c)
WARMLEY 215.57c (128m 9c)

South Junction (0m 32c) Ex-Station Junction
South Junction 214m 65c (125m 16c) S.B. 214m 64c (125m 16c)

SISTON

ABSON

End of M.R. (124m 60c)
Junction of Carsons Ld (Packers) Loop Siding 124m 18c (124m 50c)
North Junction 214m 14c (124m 46c) S.B. 214m 13c (124m 45c)
MANGOTSFIELD
NORTH JUNCTION

SHORTWOOD

PUCKLECHURCH

Sharwood Brick & Tile Cos Siding & S.B. 213m 25c (123m 57c)

Parkfield Colliery Sidings South Pt 213m 4c (123m 36c)

Parkfield Colliery Sidings North Pt 212m 44c (122m 76c)

STATION 214.54c (125m 6c)
Station Junction S.B. (125m 10c)
Sums Siding S.B. (125m 31c)
Station Junction U.Junction (125m 43c)

From Bristol

From Bristol

To Gloucester

2c

69c

40c

40c

38c

5c

43c

4c

25c

72c

SHEET 53ᴬ

ENLARGEMENT
— OF —
BATH

1918.

BATH
MIDLAND STATION
224ᴹ28ᶜ (134ᴹ60ᶜ)
G.W. STATION

CHARLCOMBE

WESTON S.B. 223ᴹ36ᶜ (133ᴹ68ᶜ)

Bath Gas Works 224ᴹ6ᶜ

WESTON

TWERTON

LYNCOMBE
AND
WIDCOMBE

RIVER AVON

From Bristol

COMBE DOWN TUNNEL 1829 YARDS
DEVONSHIRE TUNNEL 447 YARDS

To BOURNEMOUTH

SOMERSET AND DORSET JOINT

Somerset and Dorset Joint Line Junction Derby, via Whitacre and Camp Hill

* MILEAGE EX LONDON ROAD JUNCTION DERBY, VIA WHITACRE AND CAMP HILL.

SHEET 60.

MONKTON
COMBE

STANTON PRIOR

ENGLISH COMBE

DORSET
To Bournemouth

ENLARGEMENT
— OF —
BRISTOL.

To Gloucester

SHEET 53A.

KINGSWOOD JUNCTION

STAPLETON

ASHLEY DOWN

STOKE BISHOP

SNEYD PARK

ST. GEORGES

LOWER EASTON

STAPLETON ROAD

ASHLEY HILL JUNCTION

MONTPELIER

REDLAND 220ᴹ54ᶜ

CLIFTON DOWN 220ᴹ54ᶜ

CLIFTON TUNNEL No.5, 1738 YARDS

CLIFTON

CLIFTONWOOD

HOTWELLS 224ᴹ21ᶜ

HOTWELLS

LAWRENCE HILL JUNCTION

ST. PHILIPS 219ᴹ32ᶜ
PASSENGER AND GOODS

BARROW LANE JUNCTION

TEMPLEMEADS
JOINT PASSENGER STATION
(G.W. AND MID.)

MARSH GOODS

TOTTERDOWN

KNOWLE

BEDMINSTER

BRISLINGTON

To RADSTOCK

GREAT WESTERN
SOMERSET

River Avon

AVONSIDE WHARF G.W. GOODS

WAPPING WHARF G.W. GOODS

LANDS MARSH G.W. GOODS

CANONS MARSH

HARBOUR

CUMBERLAND BASIN

FLOATING BASIN

CLIFTON SUSPENSION BRIDGE

CLIFTON BRIDGE STATION

LONG ASHTON

ASHTON JUNCTION

To Main Line

From Portishead

From Monmouth

SNEYD PARK JUNCTION

G.W. AND MID. AND AVONMOUTH

On Avonside Branch
Union Road Level Crossing (129ᴹ62ᶜ)
Barton Vale do. (129ᴹ64ᶜ)
Barton Road do. (129ᴹ67ᶜ)
Avon Street do. (129ᴹ75ᶜ)

* Mileage Ex London Road Junction Derby, via Whitacre and Camp Hill

The continuous Distances not in brackets are from ST. PANCRAS PASSENGER STATION by the Shortest Route.

* Mileage Ex London Road Junction Derby, via Whitacre and Camp Hill.

The continuous Distances in brackets represent the Mile Post Mileage.

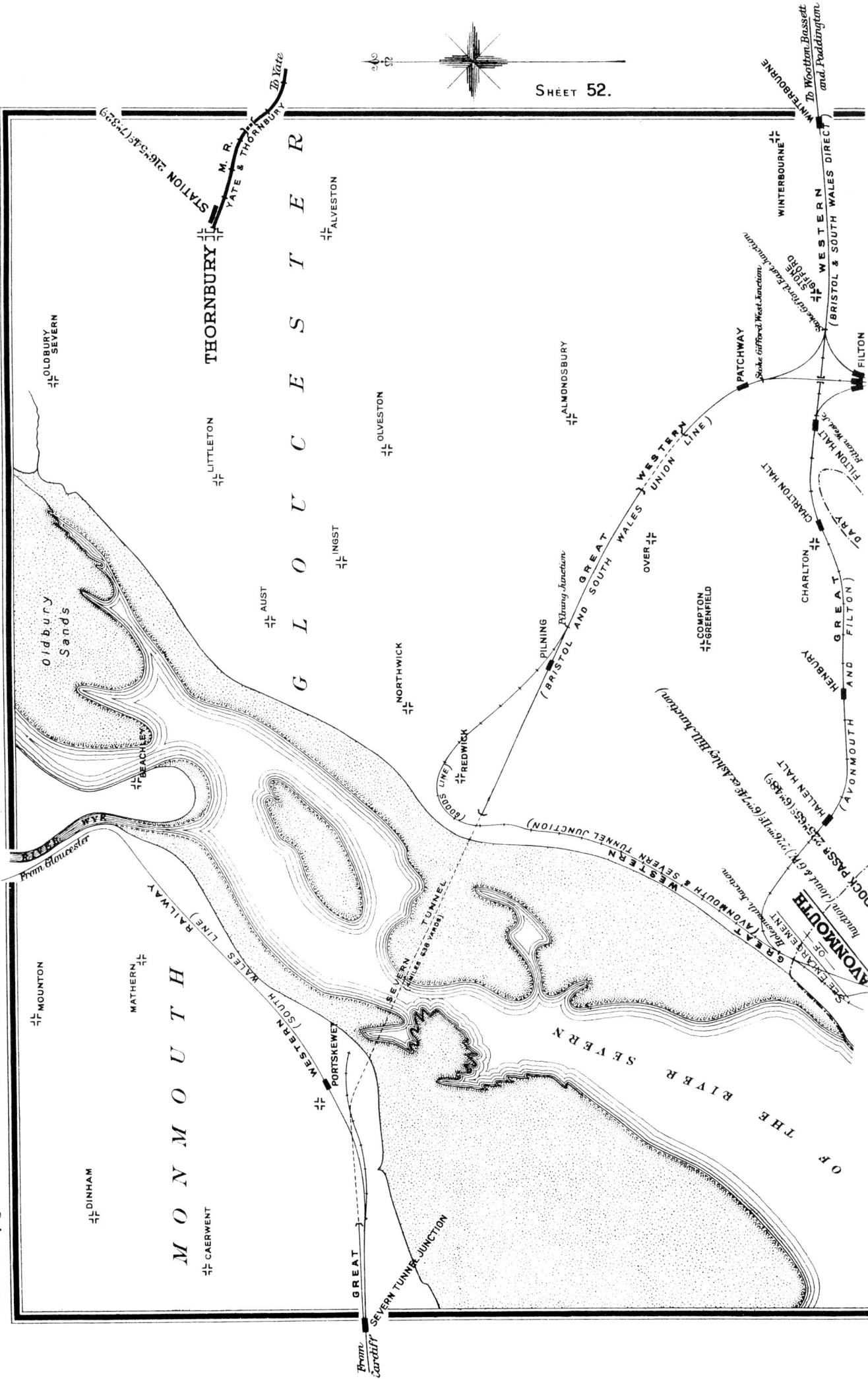

MIDLAND RAILWAY DISTANCE DIAGRAM. SCALE 1 INCH TO 1 MILE.

BRISTOL DISTRICT.

BOOK No 76

SHEET 51A

SHEET 52.

To Yate

M. R.

STATION 216m 54c (7=329)

YATE & THORNBURY

THORNBURY

G L O U C E S T E R

OLDBURY SEVERN

LITTLETON

ALVESTON

OLVESTON

INGST

AUST

NORTHWICK

ALMONDSBURY

COMPTON GREENFIELD

To Wootton Bassett and Paddington

To Wootton Bassett and Paddington

WINTERBOURNE

WINTERBOURNE

GREAT WESTERN (BRISTOL & SOUTH WALES DIRECT)

STOKE GIFFORD

Stoke Gifford West Junction

PATCHWAY

FILTON

FILTON HALT

Filton West Jc.

CHARLTON HALT

DARY

CHARLTON

GREAT (AVONMOUTH AND FILTON)

HENBURY

HALLEN HALT

DOCK PASS

AVONMOUTH

(BRISTOL AND SOUTH WALES UNION LINE)

PILNING

Pilning Junction

OVER

(GOODS LINE)

FREDWICK

GREAT WESTERN (AVONMOUTH & SEVERN TUNNEL JUNCTION)

SEVERN TUNNEL

River Wye

From Gloucester

Oldbury Sands

BEACHLEY

M O N M O U T H

MOUNTON

MATHERN

DINHAM

CAERWENT

SOUTH WALES LINE

WESTERN (SOUTH WALES) RAILWAY

PORTSKEWETT

GREAT

SEVERN TUNNEL JUNCTION

From Cardiff

THE RIVER SEVERN

T H E   R I V E R   S E V E R N

O F

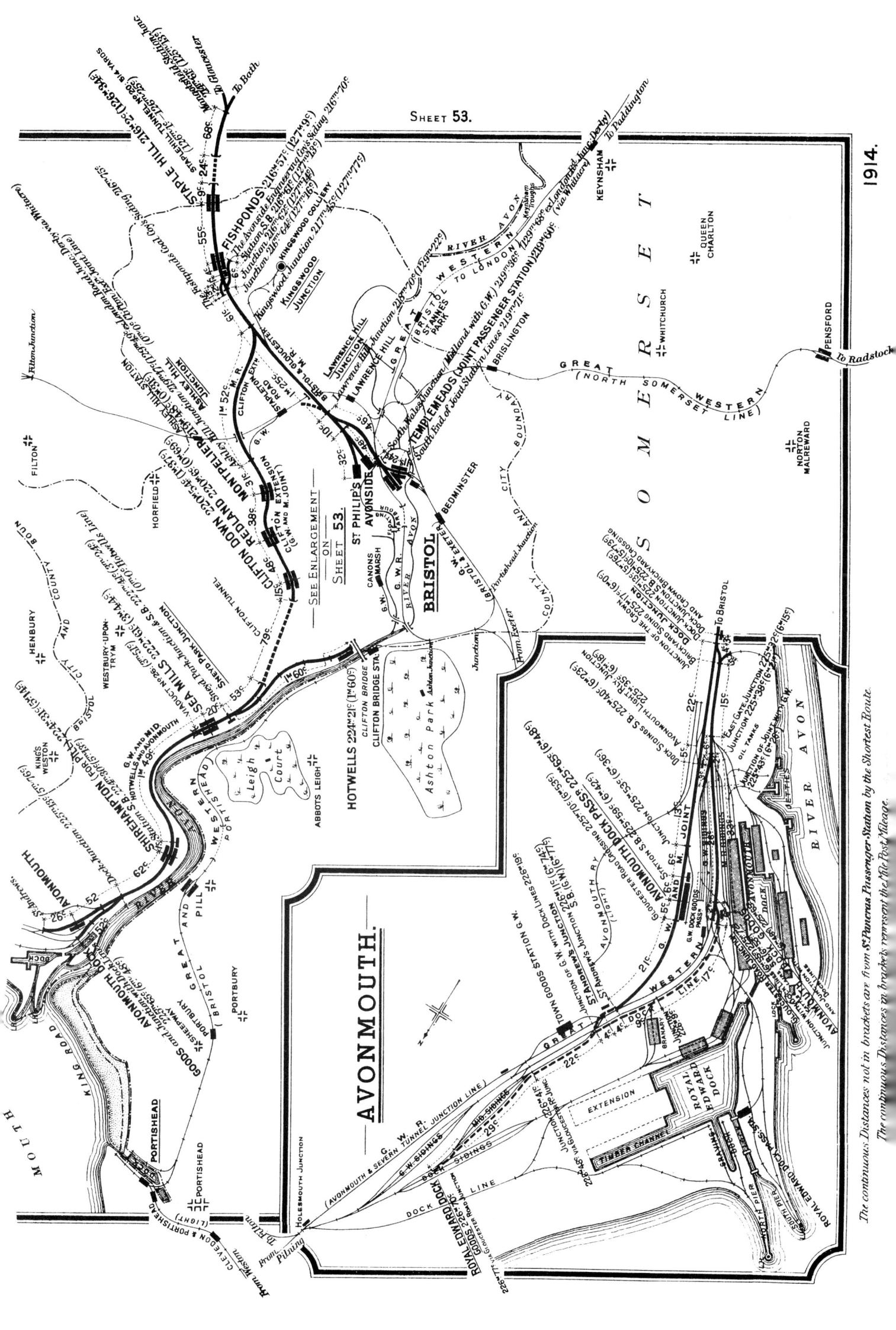

1914.

To Bath

To Gloucester

FISHPONDS 216m.57c. (127m.9½c.)
The Avonside Engineering Co's. Siding 216m.70c.
Station S.B. 216m.65c. (127m.18c.)
Junction 216m.72c. (127m.25c.)
Kingswood Junction 217m.5c. (127m.36½c.)

STAPLE HILL 216m.9½c. (126m.42c.)
STAPLE HILL TUNNEL No. 2 216m.7½c. (126m.71c.) Siding 216m.75c.
STAPLE HILL TUNNEL No. 1 216m.5c. (126m.54c.) 814 yards

Kingswood Junction

Kingswood Colliery

To Paddington

KEYNSHAM

Keynsham Troughs

QUEEN CHARLTON

WHITCHURCH

NORTON MALREWARD

PENSFORD

To Radstock

G R E A T   W E S T E R N

RIVER   AVON

BRISTOL ST. ANNES PARK

Lawrence Hill Junction 218m.70c. (129m.22c.)

LAWRENCE HILL JUNCTION

LAWRENCE HILL

Bristol Gloucester

TO LONDON (129m.66c.)

TEMPLE MEADS JOINT PASSENGER STATION 219m.30c.
South Wales Junction, Midland with G.W. 219m.38c.
South End of Joint Station Lines 219m.71c.

BRISLINGTON

G R E A T   (N O R T H   S O M E R S E T   L I N E)   W E S T E R N

S O M E R S E T

Filton Junction

FILTON

ASHLEY HILL 217m.43c. (128m.6½c.) Station 217m.39c.
MONTPELIER 220m.34c. (0m.59c.)
CLIFTON DOWN 220m.45c. (0m.49c.)
REDLAND 220m.34c. (0m.69c.)
CLIFTON EXTENSION (G.W. AND M. JOINT)

CLIFTON TUNNEL

HENBURY

WESTBURY-UPON-TRYM

HORFIELD

KING'S WESTON

VIADUCT No. 36 (3m.5½c.)
Shirehampton Station 223m.63c. (3m.4½c.)
SEA MILLS 222m.43c. (3m.44c.)
SNEYD PARK JUNCTION
G.W. AND M. JOINT HOTWELLS 1m.49c. AND AVONMOUTH

See Enlargement on Sheet 53.

ST PHILIP'S AVONSIDE

CANONS MARSH

BRISTOL

G.W.R.

RIVER AVON

G.W. & EXETER JUNCTION

BEDMINSTER

From Exeter

(Portishead Junction)

HOTWELLS 224m.21c. (1m.60c.)
CLIFTON BRIDGE STA.

Leigh Court

Ashton Park

Ashton Junction

SHIREHAMPTON S.B. 223m.63c.

G.W. AND MID.

RIVER   AVON   PILL

PORTBURY

(BRISTOL PORT AND PIER)

ABBOTS LEIGH

CITY AND COUNTY BOUNDARY

Holesmouth Junction

Pilning

From Pilning

AVONMOUTH

Avonmouth Junction

KING ROAD

AVONMOUTH DOCK

GOODS

PORTISHEAD

PORTISHEAD

(LIGHT)

(Avonmouth & Severn Tunnel Junction Line)

G. W. R.

ROYAL EDWARD DOCK GOODS 226m.70c.

TOWN GOODS STATION G.W. with Dock Lines 226m.19c.

ST. ANDREW'S JUNCTION S.B. (G.W.) 226m.11c. (6m.74½c.)

DOCK LINE

G.W. SIDINGS

MID. SIDINGS

DOCK SIDINGS

Junction of G.W. with Dock Lines 226m.11c. (6m.74½c.)

TIMBER CHANNEL

EXTENSION

ROYAL EDWARD DOCK

GRANARY

G.W. DOCK GOODS PASS.

AVONMOUTH

AVONMOUTH DOCK

JUNCTION of OIL SIDINGS

EAST GATE JUNCTION 225m.36c. (6m.49c.)
AVONMOUTH LIGHT RLY JUNCTION 225m.40c.
JUNCTION of the CROWN BRICKYARD CROSSING

Dock Junction S.B. 225m.10c. (6m.39c.)

Dock Sidings S.B. 225m.40c. (6m.35c.)

Avonmouth S.B. 225m.65c. (6m.53c.)

AVONMOUTH DOCK PASS. 225m.65c.

ROYAL EDWARD DOCK

NORTH PIER

SOUTH PIER

To Bristol

To Filton

The continuous Distances not in brackets are from St. Pancras Passenger Station by the Shortest Route.
The continuous Distances in brackets represent the Mile Post Mileage.

MIDLAND RAILWAY DISTANCE DIAGRAM. SCALE 1 INCH TO 1 MILE.
GREAT WESTERN RAILWAY.
LEDBURY DISTRICT.

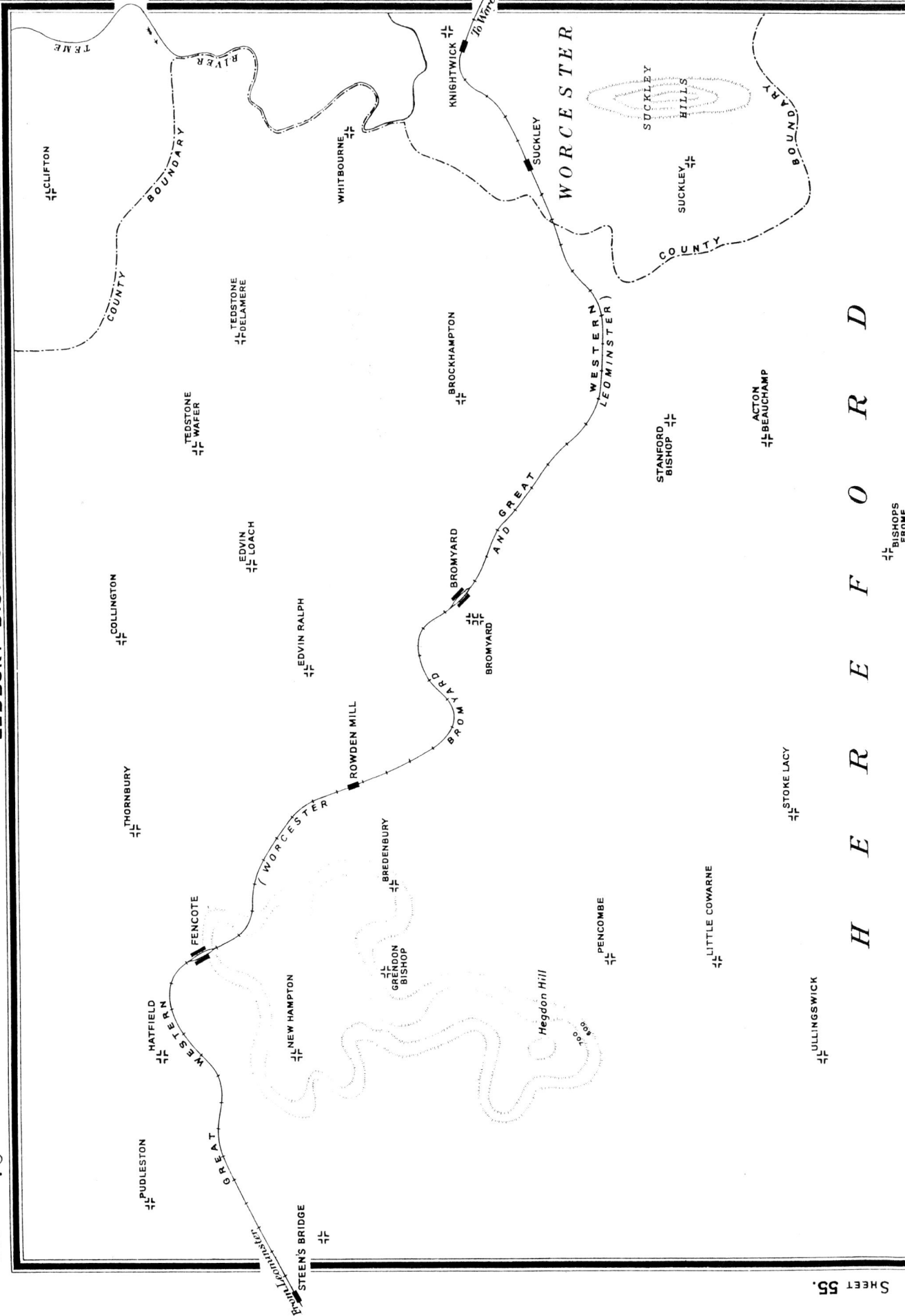

BOOK No. 76

TEME

RIVER TEME

CLIFTON

BOUNDARY

COUNTY

RIVER

To Worcester

KNIGHTWICK

WHITBOURNE

SUCKLEY

WORCESTER

SUCKLEY HILLS

SUCKLEY

BOUNDARY

COUNTY

TEDSTONE DELAMERE

TEDSTONE WAFER

BROCKHAMPTON

WESTERN

GREAT AND

LEOMINSTER

STANFORD BISHOP

ACTON BEAUCHAMP

EDVIN LOACH

COLLINGTON

EDVIN RALPH

BROMYARD

BROMYARD

BROMYARD

WESTERN

BISHOPS FROME

H E R E F O R D

STOKE LACY

ROWDEN MILL

WORCESTER

THORNBURY

BREDENBURY

GRENDON BISHOP

NEW HAMPTON

Hegdon Hill

LITTLE COWARNE

PENCOMBE

FENCOTE

HATFIELD

ULLINGSWICK

PUDLESTON

GREAT

From Leominster

STEEN'S BRIDGE

CRADLEY

COLWALL 167ᴹ64ᶜ

COLWALL

CODDINGTON

BOSBURY

Ledbury Tunnel 1320 YARDS

4ᴹ17ᶜ

Gloucester Lane Junction 171ᴹ55ᶜ

LEDBURY 171ᴹ21ᶜ

VIADUCT

LEDBURY

EASTNOR

Eastnor Park

Castle

BOUNDARY

BROMSBERROW

DONNINGTON

COUNTY

NEWTOWN

GREAT WESTERN & LEDBURY (GLOUCESTER) BRANCH

From Gloucester

CASTLE FROME

CANON FROME

MUNSLEY

ASHPERTON 175ᴹ69ᶜ

ASHPERTON

WESTERN AND HEREFORD RAILWAY 3ᴹ57ᶜ

LINE

PIXLEY

PUTLEY

LITTLE MARCLE

PRESTON

GLOUCESTER

MUCH COWARNE

STRETTON GRANDISON

YARKHILL

STOKE EDITH 178ᴹ17ᶜ

GREAT WESTERN 3ᴹ12ᶜ

MALVERN 2ᴹ35ᶜ

TARRINGTON

WESTHIDE

WESTON BEGGARD

STOKE EDITH

DORMINGTON

WOOLHOPE

OGLE PYCHARD

WITHINGTON 181ᴹ29ᶜ

From Hereford

WITHINGTON

HAMPTON BISHOP

MORDIFORD

FOWNHOPE

RIVER WYE

From Hereford HOLME LACY

GREAT WESTERN (HEREFORD, ROSS & GLOUCESTER)

To Gloucester

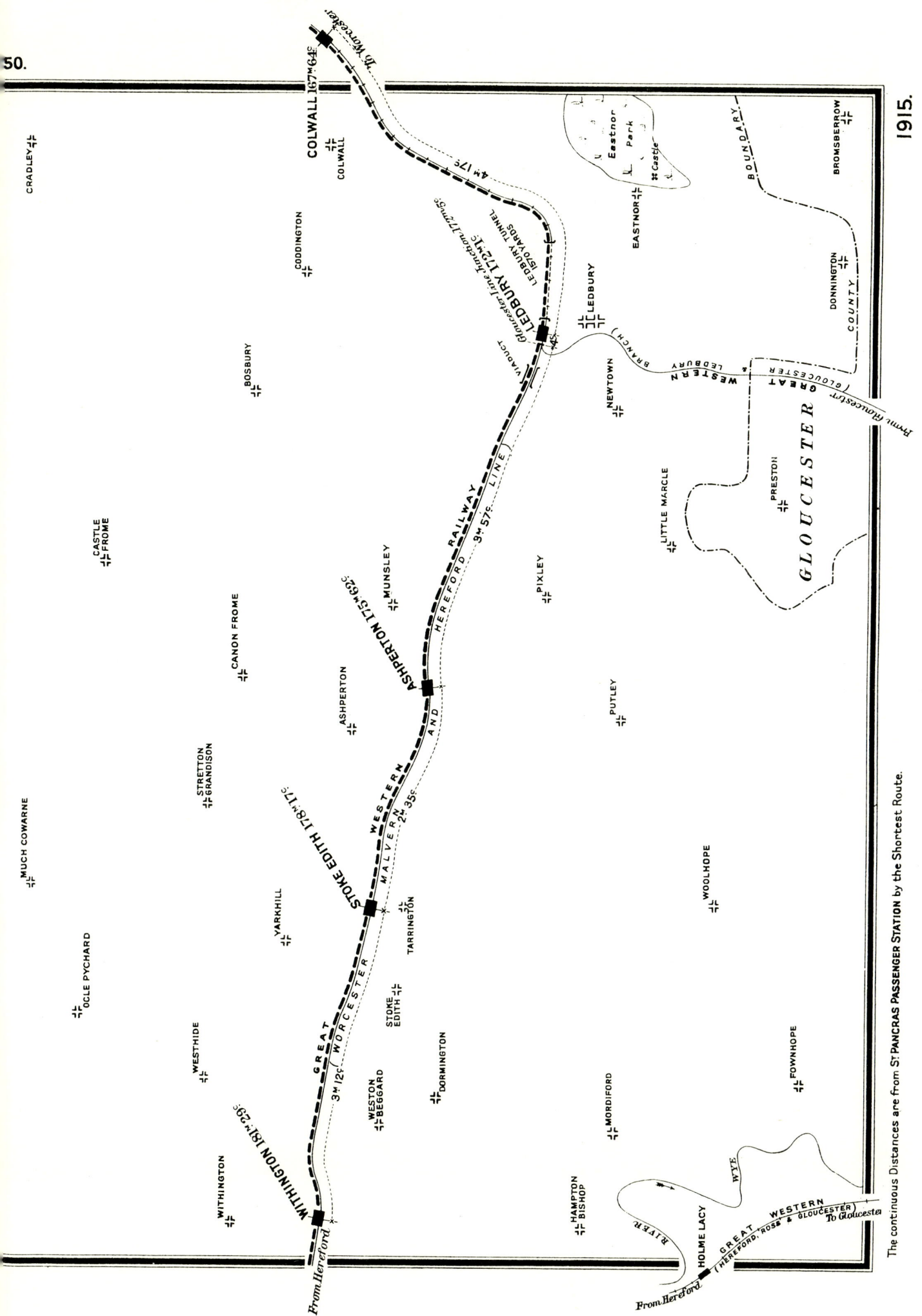

The continuous Distances are from St PANCRAS PASSENGER STATION by the Shortest Route.

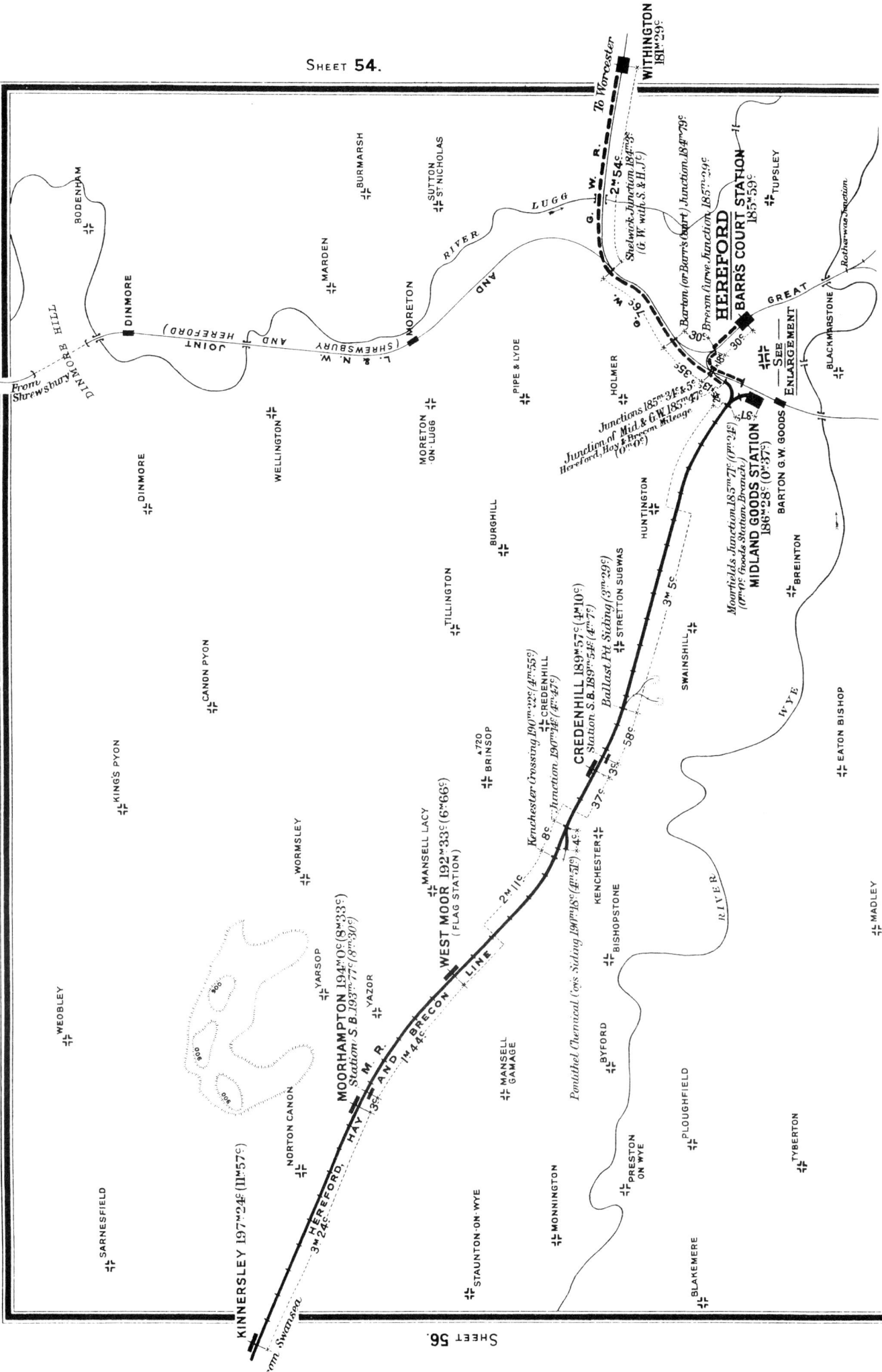

MIDLAND RAILWAY DISTANCE DIAGRAM. SCALE 1 INCH TO 1 MILE.
HEREFORD DISTRICT.

WITHINGTON 181ᴹ29ᶜ
To Worcester
G. W. R.
2ᴹ54ᶜ
Shelwick Junction 184ᴹ63ᶜ
(G. W. with S. & H. Jᵗ)
Barton (or Barr's Court) Junction 184ᴹ79ᶜ
Breeon Curve Junction 185ᴹ29ᶜ
HEREFORD
BARR'S COURT STATION 185ᴹ59ᶜ
TUPSLEY
30ᶜ
35ᶜ
Junctions 185ᴹ34ᶜ & 5ᶜ
Junction of Mid. & G.W. 185ᴹ47ᶜ
Hereford, Hay & Breeon Mileage
(0ᴹ0ᶜ)
HOLMER
30ᶜ
GREAT
Rotherwas Junction
BLACKMARSTONE
SEE ENLARGEMENT
Moorfields Junction 185ᴹ71ᶜ (0ᴹ24ᶜ)
(0ᴹ0ᶜ Goods Station Branch)
MIDLAND GOODS STATION 186ᴹ28ᶜ (0ᴹ57ᶜ)
Barton G.W. GOODS
G.W. 3ᴹ76ᶜ
PIPE & LYDE
RIVER LUGG
HUNTINGTON
BREINTON
3ᴹ 5ᶜ
BURGHILL
SWAINSHILL
TILLINGTON
Kenchester Crossing 190ᴹ02ᶜ (4ᴹ55ᶜ)
Junction 190ᴹ34ᶜ (4ᴹ47ᶜ)
CREDENHILL
Station S.B. 189ᴹ54ᶜ (4ᴹ7ᶜ)
CREDENHILL 189ᴹ57ᶜ (4ᴹ10ᶜ)
8ᶜ
37ᶜ
3ᶜ
58ᶜ
KENCHESTER
Ballast Pit Siding (3ᴹ29ᶜ)
STRETTON SUGWAS
BISHOPSTONE
Pontithel Chemical Cos Siding 191ᴹ18ᶜ (4ᴹ51ᶜ)
4ᶜ
BYFORD
CANON PYON
▲720
BRINSOP
KING'S PYON
MANSELL LACY
WEST MOOR 192ᴹ33ᶜ (6ᴹ66ᶜ)
(FLAG STATION)
WORMSLEY
2ᴹ11ᶜ
MANSELL GAMAGE
YARSOP
YAZOR
MOORHAMPTON 194ᴹ0ᶜ (8ᴹ33ᶜ)
Station S.B. 193ᴹ77ᶜ (8ᴹ30ᶜ)
M. R.
HEREFORD, HAY AND BRECON LINE
194ᴹ4ᶜ
3ᶜ
WEOBLEY
PLOUGHFIELD
PRESTON ON WYE
MONNINGTON
NORTON CANON
SARNESFIELD
STAUNTON-ON-WYE
TYBERTON
MADLEY
EATON BISHOP
RIVER WYE
BLAKEMERE
KINNERSLEY 197ᴹ24ᶜ (11ᴹ57ᶜ)
3ᴹ24ᶜ
from Swansea

DINMORE HILL
DINMORE
From Shrewsbury
JOINT (HEREFORD) AND
L. & N. W. (SHREWSBURY) AND
RIVER LUGG
MORETON
MORETON ON-LUGG
WELLINGTON
DINMORE
BODENHAM
BURMARSH
MARDEN
SUTTON ST NICHOLAS

HEREFORD.

1915.

WESTERN (HEREFORD ROSS & GLOUCESTER) To Gloucester

HOLME LACY

DINDOR

LOWER BULLINGHAM

BULLINGHAM

Red Hill Junction

L AND N. W.

WESTERN

GREAT

RedHill Junction

WESTERN

ACONBURY

CALLOW

DEWSALL

CLEHONGER

ALLENSMORE

GREAT (NEWPORT)

TRAM INN

THRUXTON

KINGSTON

KILPECK

ST DEVEREUX

WESTERN

AND

ABERGAVENNY

WORMBRIDGE

PONTRILAS

KENTCHURCH

MONNOW

GROSMONT

RIVER MONNOW

ROWLSTONE

EWYAS HAROLD

DULAS

BACTON

ABBEYDORE

WESTERN VALLEY LINE)

GREAT (GOLDEN

BACTON

LLANCILLO

GREAT HEREFORD COUNTY BOUNDARY NEWPORT

From Newport

VOWCHURCH

From Hay

MONMOUTH

Hereford detail

Barton & Brecon Curve Junc.
Junction of S & H. J.T. with G.W. 185ᴹ34ᶜ
Junction for M.R. 185ᴹ35ᶜ
Junction of Mid. and G.W. 185ᴹ47ᶜ
Hereford, Hay and Brecon Line Mileage (0·05)
From Brecon & Brecon Branch M.R.

Moorfields Junction 185ᴹ75ᶜ (0ᴹ28ᶜ)
Single Line Junction S.B. and
Moorfields Junction Branch Junction 185ᴹ71ᶜ (0ᴹ24ᶜ)
Goods Station Branch (0ᴹ0ᶜ Goods Station Branch)

MIDLAND GOODS STATION (MOORFIELDS) 186ᴹ28ᶜ (0ᴹ37ᶜ)

BARTON GOODS STATION (G.W.R.)

G.W. ENGINE SHED

GAS WORKS

WORCESTER SIDINGS Junc. 185ᴹ49ᶜ

Mid. Engine Shed

Cathedral

HEREFORD

RIVER WYE

GREAT

WESTERN

L AND N.W.R. (ROTHERWAS CURVE)

ROTHERWAS JUNCTION

Red Hill Junction

FROM NEWPORT

To Gloucester

To Worcester

To Shrewsbury

G.W.R. Ct. of G.W.R.

S AND H. JOINT Ct.

S. AND H. JT.

Shelwick Junction 184ᴹ3ᶜ (G.W. with S & H.JOINT)

Barton or Barrs Court Junction 184ᴹ79ᶜ (S. & H. JOINT with G.W.)

Brecon Curve Junction 185ᴹ29ᶜ

BARRS COURT STATION 185ᴹ59ᶜ (G.W. AND L. AND N.W. JOINT) Junction of S & H. J.T. with G.W.R.

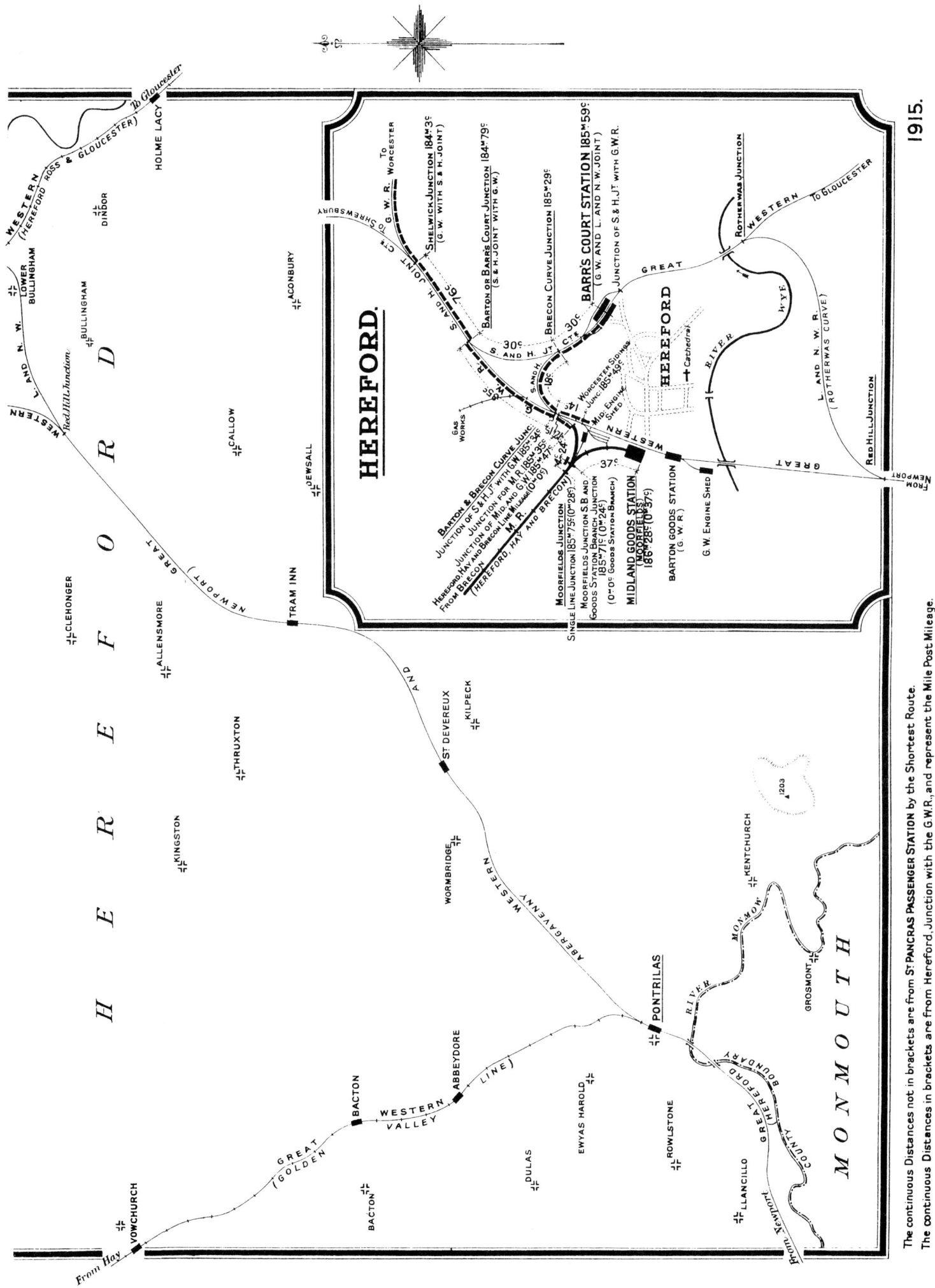

The continuous Distances not in brackets are from Sᵀ PANCRAS PASSENGER STATION by the Shortest Route.

The continuous Distances in brackets are from Hereford, Junction with the G.W.R., and represent the Mile Post Mileage.

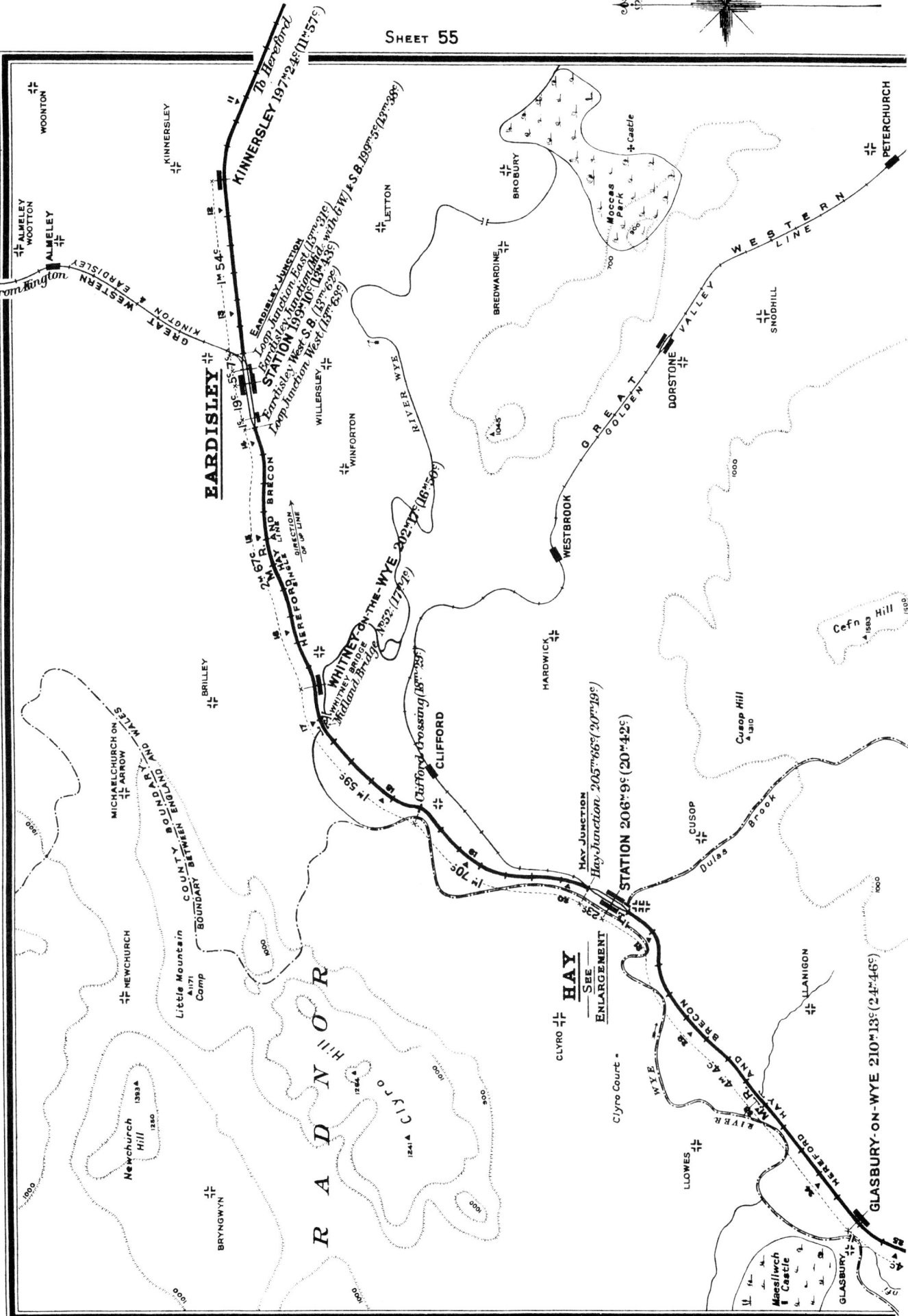

Midland Railway Distance Diagram. Scale 1 Inch to 1 Mile.

Hay District.

Book Nº 76

1921.

To Pontrilas

TURNSTONE

H E R E F O R D

CRASWALL

Black Hill

BOUNDARY   BETWEEN   ENGLAND   AND   WALES

B R E C K N O C K

B L A C K   MOUNTAINS

LLANEUEU

2306

2338

2091

2228

2000

2000

1500

1000

THREE COCKS

PONTITHEL

CAMBRIAN
From Llanidloes
& Builth

From Brecon

LLLIAN

THREE COCKS JUNCTION
Junction of Mid: with Cambrian 21ᴹ 17ᶜ 25ᵞ 50ᵞ.

STATION 211ᴹ 46ᶜ.
Three Cocks Junction S.B. 211ᴹ 47ᶜ.
Three Cocks Junction 211ᴹ 52ᶜ.

Acts of Parliament.

Hereford, Hay and Brecon Line.
1859 (H.H.& B. Coy.) Incorporation Act. - Agt with GW & L&NW. 21.5.91.
1874 (M.R.) Vesting in Mid. by Lease -1886 Dissolution.
(Other Acts 1860, 82, 63, 65 - Hay Tramway Bill 12, 60.)
Opened Hereford-Eardisley 29.6.63 - Eardisley-Three Cocks - 64.

Kington and Eardisley Line.
1862 (K & E Coy.) Incorporation Act. (Kington-Tramroad 1818)
1873 Powers as to Eardisley Station.
1897 (G.W.) Vesting Act. (Other Acts 1865, 8, 71, 5, 88 G.W.)
Opened to Eardisley 3, 8, 74.

Golden Valley Line.
1876-7 (G.V. Coy.) Incorporation and Hay Extension.
1899 Vesting in G.W.R. (Other Acts 1882, 4, 7, 9, 91.)
Agreement G.V.Coy. with M.R. of 30. 7.1888.
Opened to Hay 27.5.89.

RIVER   MONNOW

LLANVEYNOE

LONGTOWN

CLODOCK

WALTERSTONE

OLDCASTLE

1000

1500

1500

COUNTY

Abbey LLANTHONY

Afon   Honddu

Grwyne   Fawr

1981

M O N M O U T H

BOUNDARY

HAY

END OF MIDLAND MAINTENANCE (20ᴹ 28ᶜ)
SINGLE LINE JUNCTION (20ᴹ 15ᶜ)
HAY JUNCTION S.B. (20ᴹ 17ᶜ)
HAY JUNCTION 205ᴹ 66ᶜ (20ᴹ 19ᶜ)
(G.W. WITH MID.)
WILLIAMS' SIDING 205ᴹ 76ᶜ (20ᴹ 29ᶜ)
WILLIAMS' TIMBER YARD
GOODS YARD
GOODS STATION
PASSENGER STATION 206ᴹ 9ᶜ (20ᴹ 42ᶜ)
STATION S.B. (20ᴹ 43ᶜ)
BOUNDARY BETWEEN ENGLAND & WALES, BRIDGE Nº60. (20ᴹ 45ᶜ)
SINGLE LINE JUNCTION (20ᴹ 51ᶜ)

RIVER   WYE

DOWN LINE
UP LINE

FROM BRECON

The continuous Distances not in brackets are from Sᵀ PANCRAS PASSENGER STATION by the Shortest Route.
The continuous Distances in brackets are from the Junction with the G.W.R. at Moorfields, Hereford,
and represent the Mile Post Mileage.

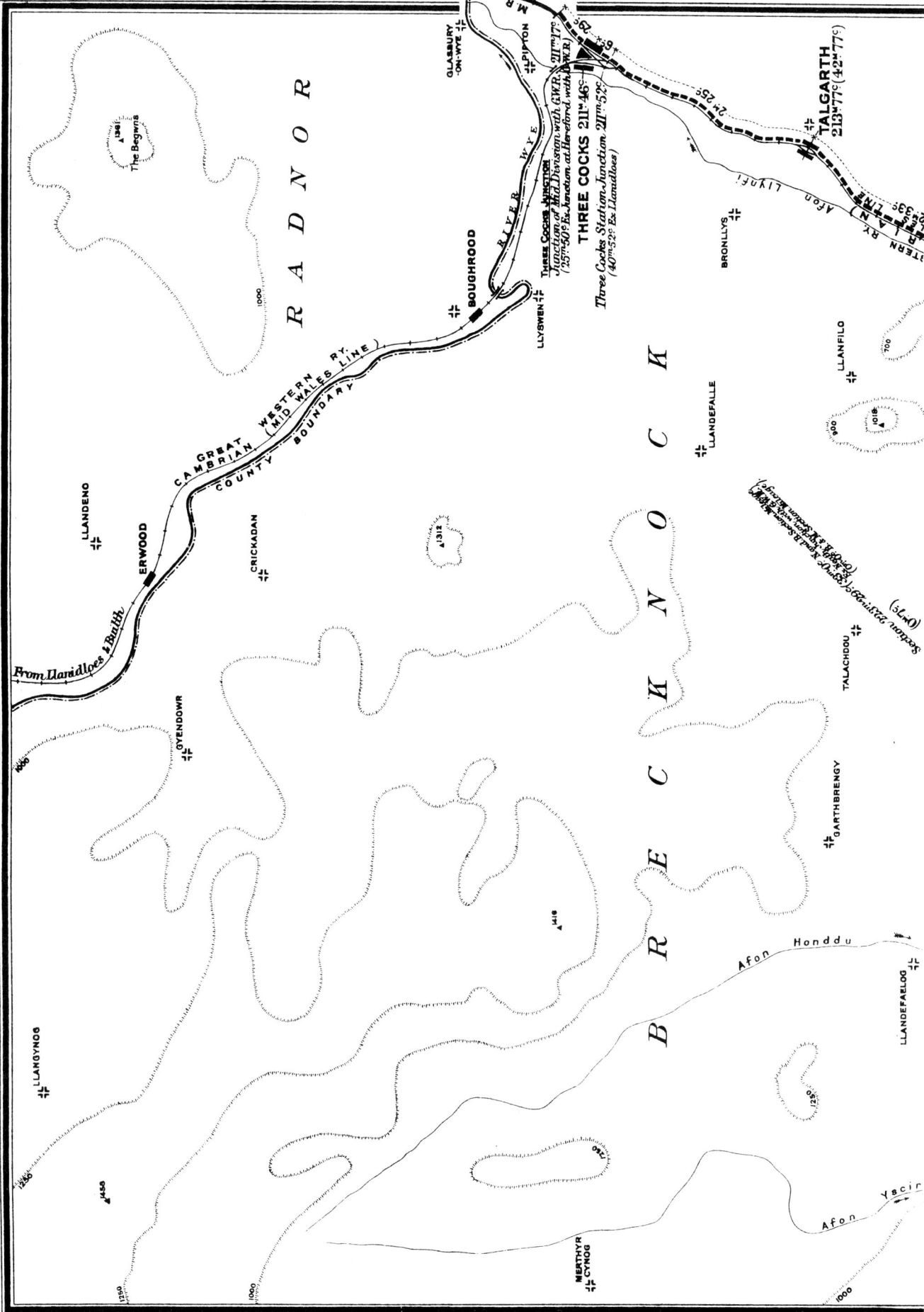

LONDON MIDLAND AND SCOTTISH RAILWAY (MIDLAND DIVISION), SCALE 1 INCH TO 1 MILE.
GREAT WESTERN RAILWAY.
BRECON DISTRICT.

BOOK Nº 76

N

R A D N O R

To Hereford

M R

GLASBURY-ON-WYE

PIPTON

RIVER WYE

Te Begwns 1361

1000

BOUGHROOD

LLYSWEN

GREAT CAMBRIAN WESTERN RY.
(MID WALES LINE)
COUNTY BOUNDARY

LLANDENO

ERWOOD

CRICKADAN

From Llanidloes & Builth

GWENDDWR

1312

1416

LLANGYNOG

1256

1450

1250

1000

Three Cocks Junction
Junction of Mid Division with G.W.R. 211ᵐ17ᶜ
(25ᵐ50ᶜ Ex Junction at Hereford with G.W.R.)

THREE COCKS 211ᵐ46ᶜ

Three Cocks Station Junction 211ᵐ52ᶜ
(40ᵐ52ᶜ Ex Llanidloes)

BRONLLYS

LLANDEFALLE

TALGARTH 213ᵐ77ᶜ (42ᵐ77ᶜ)

24ᵐ25ᶜ

Afon Llynfi

LLANFILO

700

900

1010

BRECKNOCK

TALACHDDU

LLANDEFAELOG

GARTHBRENGY

Afon Honddu

MERTHYR CYNOG

Afon Yscir

1250

1000

1000

The continuous Distances not in brackets are from St PANCRAS PASSENGER STATION by the Shortest Route.

The continuous Distances in brackets represent the Mile Post Mileage.

1923.

Sheet 58.

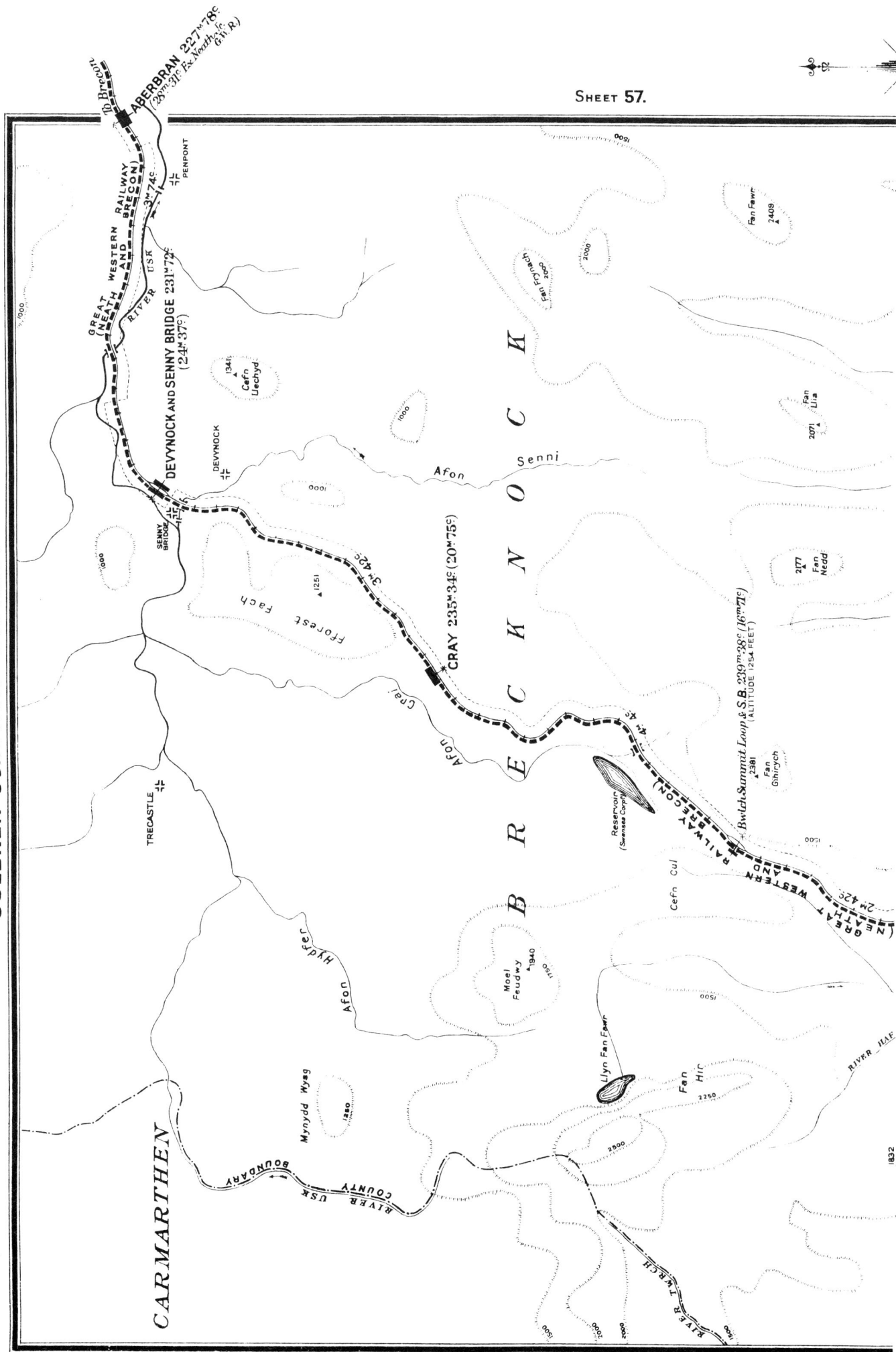

SHEET **58.**
(Seventh Edition.)

LONDON MIDLAND AND SCOTTISH RAILWAY (MIDLAND DIVISION), SCALE 1 INCH TO 1 MILE.
GREAT WESTERN RAILWAY.
COLBREN JUNCTION DISTRICT.

BOOK Nº 76

ABERBRAN 227ᴹ·78ᶜ·
(28ᴹ·31ᶜ· Ex North Jc.
G.W.R.)
To Brecon

GREAT WESTERN RAILWAY
(GREAT NEATH AND BRECON)
RIVER USK
PENPONT
3ᴹ·74ᶜ·

DEVYNOCK AND SENNY BRIDGE 231ᴹ·72ᶜ·
(24ᴹ·37ᶜ·)

DEVYNOCK

Cefn
Uechyd 1347

SENNY
BRIDGE

1000

TRECASTLE

Fforest Fach

1251

3ᴹ·42ᶜ·

CRAY 235ᴹ·34ᶜ· (20ᴹ·75ᶜ·)

Afon Cray

Afon Senni

1000

Fan Frynach

2000

1500

Fan Fawr
2409

Fan
Llia
2071

277
Fan
Nedd

Fan
Gihirych
2381

Bwlch Summit Loop & S.B. 239ᴹ·28ᶜ·(16ᴹ·T₁ᶜ·)
(ALTITUDE 1254 FEET)

Reservoir
(Swansea Corp⁽ᴺ⁾)

Cefn Cul

GREAT WESTERN AND BRECON RAILWAY

2ᴹ·42ᶜ·

1500

B   R   E   C   K   N   O   C   K

Afon Hydfer

Moel
Feudwy
1940

1750

Llyn Fan Fawr

Fan
Hir
2250

2500

Mynydd Wysg

1380

1500

1500

2000

RIVER TWRCH

RIVER ILAF

1832

CARMARTHEN

USK COUNTY BOUNDARY

RIVER

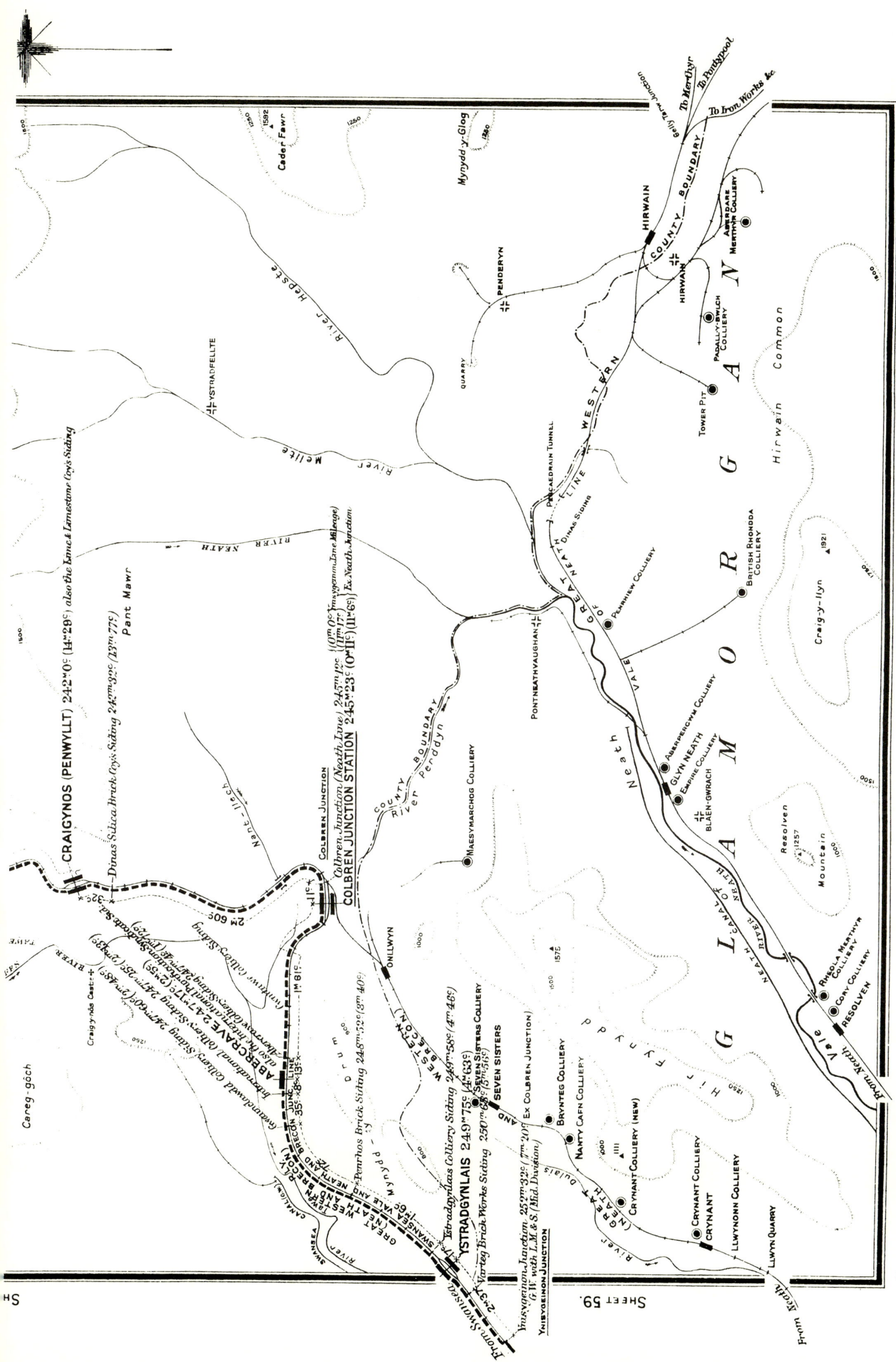

1923.

The continuous Distances not in brackets are from ST. PANCRAS PASSENGER STATION by the Shortest Route.
The continuous Distances in brackets represent the GREAT WESTERN RY (NEATH & BRECON RAILWAY SECTION) Mile Post Mileage.

To Merthyr
To Pontypool
To Iron Works &c
Gelli Tarw Junction

HIRWAIN
COUNTY BOUNDARY
HIRWAIN
PENDERYN
ABERDARE
MERTHYR COLLIERY
PADELLY-BWLCH COLLIERY
QUARRY
TOWER PIT
Hirwain Common
Mynydd-y-Glog
Ceder Fawr
1592
1250
1250
1350
1250

YSTRADFELLTE
River Hepste
River Mellte
Pant Mawr
RIVER NEATH

GREAT WESTERN LINE
DINAS SIDING
PENCAEDRAIN TUNNEL
PLENVIEW COLLIERY
PONTNEATHVAUGHAN

G L A M O R G A N

VALE OF NEATH
BRITISH RHONDDA COLLIERY
Craig-y-llyn
1921
ABERPERGWM COLLIERY
GLYN NEATH
EMPIRE COLLIERY
BLAEN-GWRACH
Neath Canal
1257
Resolven Mountain

RHEOLA MERTHYR COLLIERY
CORY COLLIERY
RESOLVEN
Neath River
Vale of Neath

Craigynos Castle
River Tawe
Careg-gôch
1600
1500

CRAIGYNOS (PENWYLLT) 242m·0c (14m·28c) also the Lime & Limestone Coys Siding
Dinas Silica Brick Coys. Siding 242m·32c (13m·77c)
Nant Llech
COLBREN JUNCTION
Colbren Junction (Neath Line) 245m·12c
Colbren Junction (Ystradgynlais Line Mileage)
COLBREN JUNCTION STATION 245m·23c (0m·11c) (11m·69c) Ex.Neath Junction
County Boundary River Penddyn
2m·60c
1m·81c
MAESYMARCHOG COLLIERY
ONLLWYN
Drum

NEATH AND BRECON (WESTERN)
ABERCRAVE 247m·75c
Abercrave Colliery (Later) Siding 247m·60c
Breconshire Colliery Junction Siding
Penrhos Brick Siding
Gurnos Colliery Siding
Ystradgynlais Colliery Siding 249m·58c (4m·46c)
SEVEN SISTERS COLLIERY
SEVEN SISTERS 248m·52c (3m·40c)
Ystradgynlais Junction 252m·32c (7m·20c) G.W. with L.M.& S.(Mid.Division)
YSTRADGYNLAIS 249m·75c (4m·63c)
Vartey Brick Works Siding 250m·15c (5m·3c)
BRYNTEG COLLIERY
NANTY CAFN COLLIERY
CRYNANT COLLIERY (NEW)
Ynisygeinon Junction 252m·37c G.W. with L.M.& S.(Mid.Division)
YNISYGEINON JUNCTION

GREAT WESTERN NEATH AND BRECON
SWANSEA VALE AND NEATH AND BRECON
SWANSEA CANAL
RIVER TAWE
1m·62c

From Swansea
From Neath

CRYNANT COLLIERY
CRYNANT
LLWYNONN COLLIERY
LLWYN QUARRY
1575
1600
1500

MIDLAND RAILWAY DISTANCE DIAGRAM. SCALE 2 INCHES TO 1 MILE.
(SWANSEA VALE LINES).

BOOK Nº **76**

SHEET **59.**
(Eighth Edition.)

BRECKNOCK

GLAMORGAN

CARMARTHEN

CARMARTHENSHIRE

Black Mountain

PENLLER-FEDWEN

RIVER TWRCH

RIVER AMAN

RIVER LLYNFELL

RIVER GWYS

RIVER GARNANT

To Black Mountain Colliery

HENLLYS COLLIERY COY'S TRAMWAY

COUNTY BOUNDARY

TWRCH BOUNDARY

CLYDACH WHARF
YSTRADGYNLAIS 249·75 (25·46°)
To BRECON

PANTMAWR COLLIERY

CLYDACH BRIDGE Nº92 (13·35°)

YSTRADGYNLAIS 254·77 (13·15°)

SWANSEA

GURNOS JUNCTION 254·0° (12·58°)
GURNOS JUNCTION
—— SEE ENLARGEMENT ——

YSTALYFERA 253·58° (12·36°)

CANAL

TRAMWAY

BLAEN-CWM COLLIERY

Phoenix Tin Plate Works

GWYS 255·62° (14·40°)
End of M.R. Gwys Bridge Nº137. (14·36°)
River Gwys Bridge Nº137. (14·36°)
Brynmorgan Crossing 255·33° (14·11°)
Brynmorgan Siding 255·29° (14·7°)
Gilwen Colliery Siding 255·24° (14·2°)
River Twrch Bridge Nº135. (14·29°)
River Twrch Bridge Nº134. (13·74°)
Cwmtwrch or Gilwen Crossing (13·53°)
Lower Cwmtwrch Crossing (13·38°)

GILWEN COLLIERY
End of M.R. 255·29° (14·7°)
Ystradowen Colliery Siding Junction 256·13° (14·71°)

GLUFACH COLLIERY
Gilfach Colliery Branch Junction 255·67° (14·45°)
Caelliau Colliery Branch Junction 255·72° (14·50°)

BRYNHENLLUSH COLLIERY 256·30° (15·8°)
The Henllys Anthracite Colliery Coy's BLACK MOUNTAIN COLLIERY SIDINGS
AND END OF MID. RAILS 256·54° (15·32°)

BRYNHENLLISH LOWER COLLIERY

End of M.R. 256·15° (14·73°)

YSTRADOWEN COLLIERY

BLAEN-WAEN SIDING 257·21° (15·79°)

CWMLLYNFELL 257·46° (16·24°)
End of M.R. 257·46° (16·24°)

GWAUN-CAE-GURWEN COLLIERY SIDINGS AND S.B. 257·58° (16·36°)
ALSO LOOP JUNCTIONS AT (16·27°) & (16·45°)
Junctions of Blaen-Cae-Gurwen and
Rhosamman Collieries 258·20° (16·78°)

RHOSAMMAN COLLIERY
End of M.R. 258·25° (17·3°)

River Aman Bridge Nº155
and County Boundary (17·15°)

BLAEN-CAE-
GURWEN COLLIERY 'YSTRAD-OWEN'

CWMLLYNFELL COLLIERY

CWMLLYNFELL COLLIERY SIDINGS JUNCTION 256·26° (15·55°)
End of M.R. 256·29° (15·79°)

River Llynfell Bridge Nº145. (15·79°)
River Llynfell Bridge Nº144. (15·79°)
River Llynfell Bridge Nº143. (15·25°)

HENDREFORGAN COLLIERY
Hendreforgan Colliery Sidings Junction 256·26° (15·55°)

GWAUN-CAE-GURWEN TRAMWAY

COLLIERY TRAMWAY

CWMTEG COLLIERY
End of M.R. 259·39° (18·17°)
Junction 259·28° (18·6°)
End of M.R. 259·30° (18·8°)

PANTYCELYN COLLIERY (AMAN ANTHRACITE)
End of M.R. 259·43° (18·21°)

MIDLAND STATION 259·44° (18·22°)

BRYNAMMAN
G.W. STATION

GREAT WESTERN BRANCH

NEW CAWDOR COLLIERY

GWAUN-CAE-GURWEN
COLLIERIES

GWAUN-CAE-GURWEN

GWAUN-CAE-GURWEN BRANCH

CWMGORSE COLLIERY

GARNANT BRANCH

GLYNBEUDY COLLIERY

Gwyn Beudy Tin Plate Works

MOYADD COLLIERY

GORS-Y-GARNANT COLLIERY

FROM PANTYFFYNON

FROM GARNANT

GREDLION CROSSING HALT

SHEET 58.

1911.

ENLARGEMENT OF

YSTALYFERA AND GURNOS JUNCTION.

TO WERNPLWMS

TO YNISCEDWYN TIN PLATE WORKS

JUNCTION 254·43ᶜ (13·21ᶜ)

Swansea Canal Bridge No 4. (13·09ᶜ)

M.R. BRANCH

REES MORGAN'S TIMBER YARD 254·42ᶜ (13·20ᶜ)

YNISCEDWYN

GURNOS JUNCTION GOODS STATION 254·14ᶜ (12·72ᶜ)

GOODS STATION JUNCTION 254·3ᶜ (12·61ᶜ)

GURNOS JUNCTION 254·0ᶜ (12·58ᶜ)

GURNOS JUNCTION S.B. 253·79ᶜ (12·57ᶜ)

BUDD'S ROAD SIDING No 118. (12·55ᶜ) AND RIVER TWRCH BRIDGE No 117. (12·55ᶜ)

JUNCTION OF TIRBACH COLLIERY & JENKINS BRICK WORKS SIDINGS 253·67ᶜ (12·45ᶜ)

END OF M.R. BUDD'S ROAD SIDING 254·5ᶜ (12·63ᶜ)
LOOP JUNCTION NORTH 253·63ᶜ (12·41ᶜ)

ENGINE SHED

SWANSEA CANAL

COLLIERY LINE

BLAEN CWM COLLIERY JUNCTION 254·37ᶜ (13·15ᶜ)

BLAEN CWM COLLIERY SIDINGS S.B. 253·31ᶜ (13·09ᶜ)

CANAL SIDINGS JUNCTION 254·28ᶜ (13·6ᶜ)

GURNOS TIN PLATE WORKS

GURNOS JUNCTION SIDINGS
AND THE GURNOS TIN PLATE & BRICK
WORKS SIDING 254·14ᶜ (12·72ᶜ)
ALSO
REES & SONS GURNOS BRICK WORKS

JENKINS GURNOS BRICK WORKS (12·50ᶜ)

TIRBACH COLLIERY (12·48ᶜ)

JUNCTION (12·48ᶜ)

RIVER

TWRCH

FROM PWLLBACH COLLY

FROM SWANSEA

YSTALYFERA 253·58ᶜ (12·36ᶜ)

STATION S.B. 253·55ᶜ (12·33ᶜ)

SWANSEA CANAL BRIDGE No 114. (12·31ᶜ)

IRON WORKS BRANCH JUNCTION 253·50ᶜ (12·28ᶜ)

LOOP JUNCTION SOUTH 253·47ᶜ (12·25ᶜ)

YSTALYFERA WORKS CROSSING S.B. (12·28ᶜ)

YSTALYFERA IRON AND TIN PLATE WORKS ALSO
THE PWLLBACH COLLIERY SIDING 253·70ᶜ (12·48ᶜ)

VIATEG BRICK WORKS SIDING

THE DIAMOND AND

THE GURNOS AND BRECON JUNCTION 1·29ᶜ

YNISCI COLLIERY 251·23ᶜ

CAMBRIAN MERCANTILE COLLIERY 251·74ᶜ

YSTALYFERA JUNCTION

YNISYGEINON JUNCTION S.B. 252·25ᶜ

YNISYGEINON JUNCTION MID.& N.& B. 252·32ᶜ ▲1160
(29·3ᶜ Ex Brecon N.& B. Junction)
(11·10ᶜ Ex Swansea)

RIVER TAWE AND SWANSEA & NEATH

PWLLBACH COLLIERY

YSTALYFERA 253·?ᶜ (12·?ᶜ)

Viaduct No 108. (12·?ᶜ)

River Bridge No 105. (11·?ᶜ)

PANTYFFYNNON

YNISYGEINON JUNCTION S.B. 252·39ᶜ (11·17ᶜ)

YNISYGEINON JUNCTION 252·32ᶜ (11·10ᶜ)

GILWEN COLLIERY

MYNYDD ALLT Y GRUG ▲1113

MYNYDD — MARCH — HYWEL

TARENI COLLIERY (PRIMROSE COLLIERY COY.)

YNISYGEINON SIDINGS S.B. 253·9ᶜ (10·33ᶜ)

YNISYGEINON SIDINGS 253·13ᶜ (10·29ᶜ)

TARENI COLLIERY SIDINGS (PRIMROSE COLLIERY COYS)
253·13ᶜ (10·29ᶜ)

JUNCTION OF CWMTAWE SIDING & YNISMEUDW FIRE CLAY WORKS 253·60ᶜ (9·62ᶜ)
WAENYCOED COLLIERY 253·77ᶜ (9·45ᶜ)

JUNCTION OF PRIMROSE COY'S WAENYCOED COLLIERY 253·77ᶜ (9·45ᶜ)

JUNCTION OF YNISMEUDW TIN PLATE WORKS SIDING 254·7ᶜ (9·35ᶜ)

END OF M.R. 254·2ᶜ (9·50ᶜ)

CEFN

CWM DU

TAWE (G.W.R. COL.)

END OF M.R. 253·62ᶜ (9·64ᶜ)

END OF M.R. 254·9ᶜ (9·49ᶜ)

YNISMEUDW OR BRYN TIN PLATE WORKS

YNISMEUDW OR BRYN TIN PLATE WORKS SIDING 254·7ᶜ

WAENYCOED OLD COLLIERY SIDING 254·42ᶜ (9·0ᶜ)
CILYBEBYLL 254·66ᶜ (8·66ᶜ)
END OF M.R. 254·66ᶜ (8·66ᶜ)
JUNCTION OF THE GELLYNUDD COLLIERY 254·61ᶜ (8·61ᶜ)

END OF M.R. 255·15ᶜ (8·41ᶜ)

JUNCTION OF GLANRHYDD (OR GLANTAWE)
IRON & TIN PLATE WORKS SIDING 255·8ᶜ (8·34ᶜ)

LLANGIWG

SWANSEA CANAL

RIVER TAWE

RHYD-Y-FRO

NORTH S.B. AND LOOP JUNCTION NORTH 255·38ᶜ (8·4ᶜ)

END OF M.R. 255·75ᶜ (7·75ᶜ)

STATION 255·47ᶜ (7·75ᶜ)

STATION S.B. 255·53ᶜ (7·69ᶜ)

"LEWIS" CHEMICAL WORKS 255·77ᶜ (7·63ᶜ)

JUNCTION OF GILBERTSONS, LEWIS', & BRYNMORSE & WERNDDU BRANCHES AND
PRIMROSE COLLIERY SIDINGS 255·68ᶜ (7·54ᶜ)
PRIMROSE COLLIERY S.B. (7·52ᶜ)

LOOP JUNCTION SOUTH 255·77ᶜ (7·51ᶜ) S.B. (7·43ᶜ)

LOOP JUNCTION SOUTH

JUNCTION OF GWYN'S DRIFT COLLIERY SIDINGS 255·79ᶜ (7·43ᶜ)

PRIMROSE COLLIERY

BRYNCOCH AND WERNDDU COLLIERIES

RHOS

COLLIERY LINE

SHEET 59ᴬ

PONTARDAWE

GILBERTSON'S PONTARDAWE STEEL & TIN PLATE WORKS 256·0ᶜ (7·66ᶜ)
JUNCTION 255·71ᶜ (7·57ᶜ)

GWYN'S DRIFT COLLIERY

END OF M.R. 255·75ᶜ

GELLYNEN COLLIERY SIDINGS 256·37ᶜ (7·15ᶜ)

GELLYNEN COLLIERY SIDINGS 256·37ᶜ (7·5ᶜ)

JUNCTION OF LLWYDCOED COLLIERY & BRICK WORKS 257·26ᶜ (6·16ᶜ)
(BOUNDARY SIDING)

GREAT WESTERN (SESSION 1911)

EGEL VALLEY

EGEL RGHEL

GREAT WESTERN RAILWAY (SESSION 1911)

UPPER CLYDACH RIVER

RIVER

MYNYDD-Y-GARTH ▲1057

MYNYDD-GELLI-ONEN

GELLYONEN COLLIERY

AERIAL LINE

G.R.E.A.T. WESTERN (SESSION 1911)

FROM SWANSEA

1153 ▲

1000

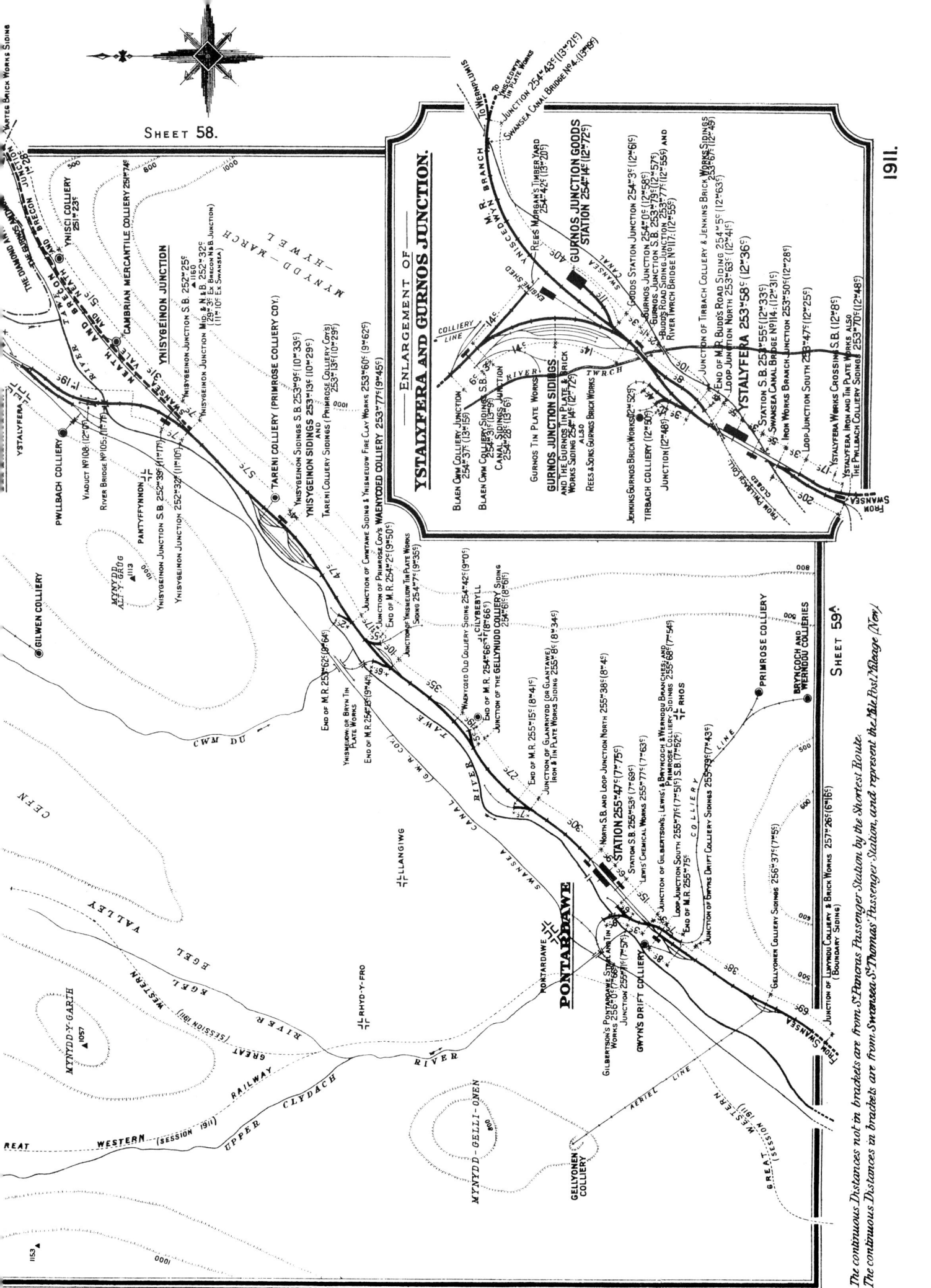

The continuous Distances not in brackets are from St Pancras Passenger Station by the Shortest Route.
The continuous Distances in brackets are from Swansea St Thomas Passenger Station, and represent the Mile Post Mileage (New).

MIDLAND RAILWAY DISTANCE DIAGRAM. SCALE 2 INCHES TO 1 MILE.
(SWANSEA VALE LINES)

SHEET 59A. (Fourth Edition.)

BOOK No. 76

SHEET 59.

To BRECON

To NEATH & MERTHYR
To PORT TALBOT
To CARDIFF

LLWYNDU COLLIERY AND BRICK WORKS
Junction (Boundary Siding) 257M 28C (6M 16C)
End of M.R. 257M 28C (6M 16C)

GLAIS JUNCTION
Glais Junction S.B. 257M 60C (5M 62C Ex Swansea)
Glais Junction S.B. and Loop Junction North 257M 61C (5M 61C)

GLAIS GOODS 257M 75C (5M 47C)
Loop Junction South 258M 1C (5M 41C)

MYNYDD DRUMAU

Way & Works Siding (5M 18C)

SISTERS PIT
End of M.R. 258M 36C (5M 10C)
Junction of Sisters Pit Siding 258M 34C (5M 8C)

BROTHERS PIT (CLOSED)
BIRCHGROVE PIT
Birchgrove Pit Junction 258M 79C (4M 43C)
BIRCHGROVE

MAIN COLLIERY
SKEWEN
DUFFRYN COLLIERY

SWANSEA VALE LINE

G.W.R. SESSION 1911
M.R.
GREAT WESTERN RAILWAY LINE

G.W. Bridge No 30A (3M 68C)
End of M.R. 259M 76C (3M 50C)
FELIN FRAN COLLIERY (GW)
Samlet Colliery Junction 259M 72C (3M 48C)

LLANSAMLET
FELIN FRAN COLLIERY (CLOSED)
Foxhole or Aber Tin Plate Works

LLANSAMLET GOODS 260M 24C (3M 18C)
End of M.R. and S.B.
Foxhole or Aber Tin Plate Works
Swansea Chemical Coy's Siding 260M 50C (2M 72C)
Swansea Vale Spelter Works & Villiers Spelter Works Junction 260M 62C (2M 60C)
Six Pit Junction 260M 71C (2M 51C)

SEE ENLARGEMENT.

CLYDACH-ON-TAWE
GLAIS PASSENGER
TAWE BRIDGE
Players Tin Plate Works
Hill's Cwm Clydach Colliery (Hills)
End of M.R. 259M 75C (5M 35C)
CWM CLYDACH GRAIGOLA COLLIERY

To PONTARDAWE AND CLYDACH MERTHYR AND CWM GRAIGOLA COLLIERIES

RIVER TAWE
G.W.R. SESSION 1911
G.W. VIADUCT No 21 (3M 78C)
G.W. Bridge No 21A (3M 67C)
Tyrcenol Siding Junction 260M 24C (3M 59C)

TAWE
CANAL (G.W. COY)
Patent Fuel Works

FROM PONTARDULAIS TUNNEL
GREAT (SESSION 1904)

MYNYDD BACH COLLIERY
LLANG YFELACH

MORRISTON BRANCH
M.R.

G.W. STATION
MORRISTON 260M 77C (3M 6C)
SEE ENLARGEMENT.

Tyrcenol Tin Plate Works
Morriston Tin Plate Works
End of M.R. 260M 31C (3M 66C)

End of M.R. 260M 65C (2M 65C)

Beaufort Tin Works Junction 261M 45C (2M 38C)
Landore Steel Works Sidings 261M 52C (2M 31C)
End of M.R. 261M 48C (2M 34C)
End of M.R. 261M 65C (1M 59C)

G.W.R. Bridge No 3 (1M 70C)
THE BRITISH MANNESMANN TUBE COY, SWANSEA HEMATITE AND S. BALDWINS LTD.
PASCOE GRENFELL & SON'S WORKS
Pascoe Grenfell Junction 262M 27C (1M 44C)
End of M.R. (1M 61C)

LANDORE
Landore Junction
Single Line Junction (1M 53C)
SINGLE LINE JUNCTION
UPPER BANK JUNCTION B.P. (1M 39C)
Upper Bank Junction 262M 8C (1M 26C)

LLANERCH COLLIERY SIDING 262M 0C (1M 46C)
Single Line Sidings S.B. 261M 44C (1M 78C)
Upper Bank Sidings S.B. 261M 52C (1M 70C)
Upper Bank Sidings 261M 60C (1M 62C)
Llanerch Colliery Junction S.B. 262M 7C (1M 34C)
ENGINE SHED

UPPER BANK 262M 10C (1M 32C)
Junction of Vivian's White Rock Silver & Lead Works 262M 42C (1M 10C)
End of M.R. 262M 44C (1M 2C)
LLANERCH SLANT
End of M.R. 262M 42C (1M 10C)
J.B. (0M 79C)

MORRISTON BRANCH
M.R.
RIVER TAWE
R.M.
WEST JUNCTION
Upper Bank Spelter Works
SIX PIT JUNCTION
M.R.
S.WALES LINE
GREAT WESTERN RAILWAY LINES

GLAMORGAN
SWANSEA DOCK JUNCTION 1911
CRYMLYN BOG

MORGAN
WESTERN LINE
GREAT

COCKETT TUNNEL
COCKETT
WIGFACH COLLIERY
FROM FISHGUARD

ENLARGEMENT OF SIX PIT JUNCTION.

To BRECON
To NEATH
Commencement of Joint Property 260M 71C (2M 51C)
Six Pit Junction 260M 71C (2M 51C)
Six Pit Junction S.B. and Junction 260M 74C (2M 48C)
VILLIERS SPELTER WORKS
G.W.R. Bridge No 20 (2M 38C)
Centre of Joint Property 261M 9C
Mid. and G.W. Agreed Junction
GLAMORGAN SPELTER COY'S
SWANSEA SMELTING WORKS 261M 10C
Dillwyn's Siding 261M 22C
End of Joint Line 261M 23C
SWANSEA VALLEY JUNCTION (G.W.R.)
Junction with G.W.R. 261M 19C

MID. AND G.W. JOINT
M.R.
FROM SWANSEA

ENLARGEMENT OF MORRISTON.

MORRISTON BRANCH
RIVER TAWE BRIDGE No 15 (3M 23C)
NORTH S.B. AND LOOP JUNCTION 260M 69C (2M 14C)
JUNCTION OF UPPER FOREST STEEL & TIN PLATE WORKS 260M 77C (3M 12C)
WORCESTER STEEL & TIN PLATE WORKS 261M 14C (3M 9C)
MORRISTON 260M 77C (3M 6C)
DYFFRYN STEEL & TIN PLATE WORKS 261M 12C (3M 7C)
JUNCTION 261M 10C (3M 5C)
JUNCTION 261M 45C (2M 79C)
SOUTH S.B. 261M 8C (2M 75C)
JUNCTION 261M 11C (2M 72C)
EVANS LOWER FOREST FOUNDRY (2M 78C)
WILLIAMS SIDING 261M 6C
G.W. STATION
JUNCTION 260M 79C (3M 4C)
STATION LOOP SOUTH (2M 69C)

FROM BRECON
TO SWANSEA
G.W.R.
FROM SWANSEA

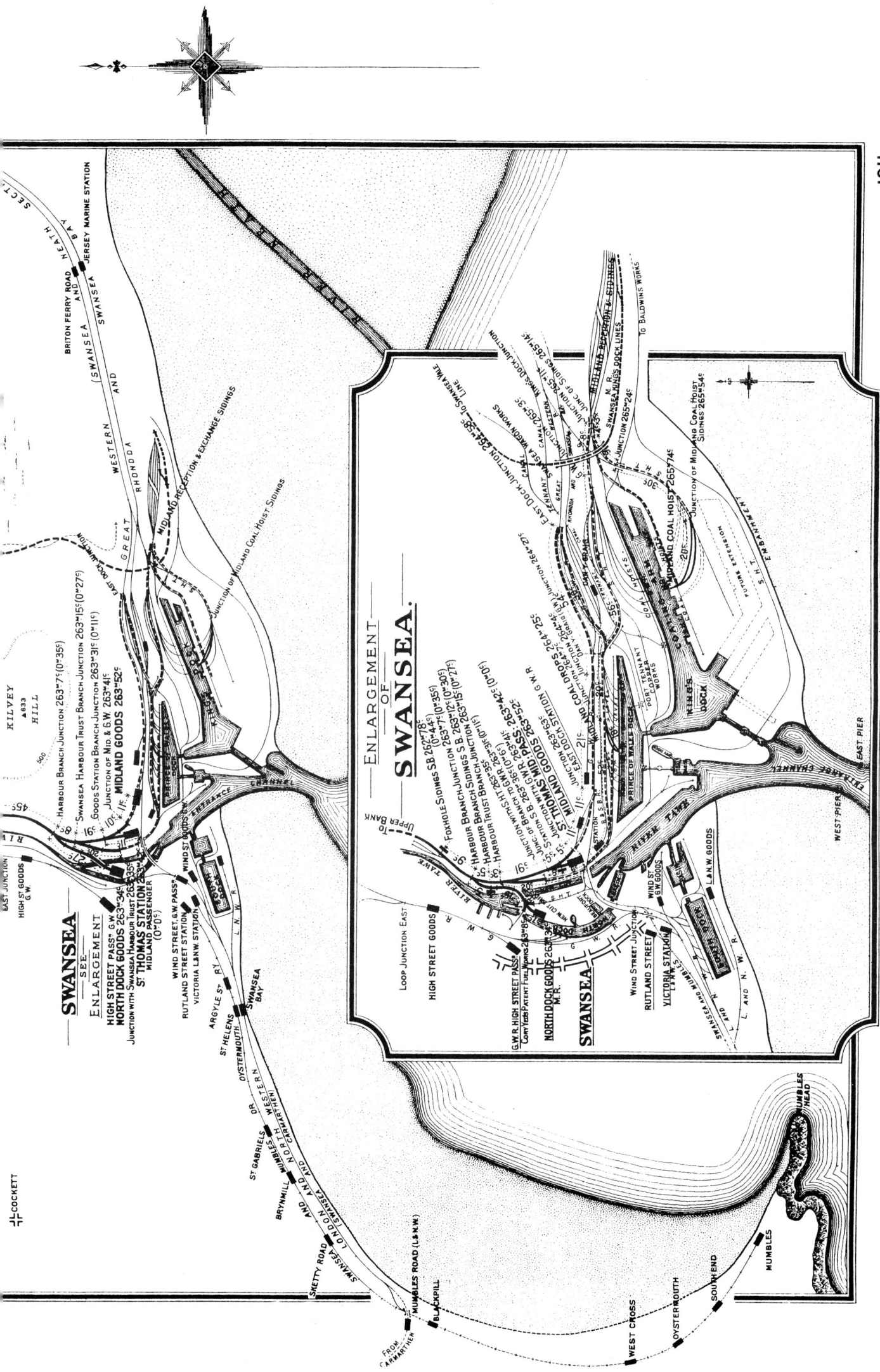

1911.

SWANSEA
SEE ENLARGEMENT

KILVEY HILL
A.633
500

COCKETT

EAST JUNCTION
HIGH ST. GOODS G.W.

Harbour Branch Junction 263ᵐ79ᶜ(0ᵐ35ᶜ)
Swansea Harbour Trust Branch Junction 263ᵐ15ᶜ(0ᵐ11ᶜ)
Goods Station Branch Junction 263ᵐ31ᶜ(0ᵐ11ᶜ)
Junction of Mid. & G.W. 263ᵐ41ᶜ

HIGH STREET PASS. G.W.
NORTH DOCK GOODS 263ᵐ34ᶜ
Junction with Swansea Harbour Trust 263ᵐ35ᶜ
ST. THOMAS STATION
MIDLAND PASSENGER
(0ᵐ0ᶜ)
MIDLAND GOODS 263ᵐ52ᶜ

WIND STREET G.W.
RUTLAND STREET STATION
VICTORIA L&N.W. STATION

MIDLAND RECEPTION & EXCHANGE SIDINGS
Junction of Midland Coal Hoist Sidings

GREAT WESTERN AND RHONDDA
MIDLAND (SWANSEA AND)

BRITON FERRY ROAD AND HEATH
SWANSEA BAY
JERSEY MARINE STATION

ENTRANCE CHANNEL

ARGYLE ST. RY.
ST. HELENS OR OYSTERMOUTH
SWANSEA BAY
ST. GABRIELS
BRYNMILL
MUMBLES (WESTERN AND NORTH CARMARTHEN)
AND AND AND
SKETTY ROAD
SWANSEA AND MUMBLES
SWANSEA LD

MUMBLES ROAD (L&N.W)
BLACKPILL
FROM CARMARTHEN

WEST CROSS
OYSTERMOUTH
SOUTHEND
MUMBLES
MUMBLES HEAD

ENLARGEMENT
— OF —
SWANSEA.

Foxhole Sidings S.B. 262ᵐ78ᶜ (0ᵐ44ᶜ)
Harbour Branch Junction 263ᵐ79ᶜ (0ᵐ30ᶜ)
Harbour Branch Sidings S.B. 263ᵐ12ᶜ (0ᵐ27ᶜ)
Harbour Trust Branch Junction 263ᵐ15ᶜ (0ᵐ11ᶜ)
Junction with S.H.T. G.W. 263ᵐ35ᶜ (0ᵐ16ᶜ)
Junction of Branch 263ᵐ35ᶜ (0ᵐ3ᵐ4ᶜ) 263ᵐ41ᶜ 263ᵐ42ᶜ (0ᵐ0ᶜ)
Junction with S.B. 263ᵐ5ᵐ8ᶜ G.W. PASS. 263ᵐ52ᶜ
Station with MID. PASS. 263ᵐ52ᶜ
ST. THOMAS MID. PASS.
ST. THOMAS GOODS 263ᵐ63ᶜ STATION G.W.R.
EAST DOCK STATION G.W.R.

LOOP JUNCTION EAST

HIGH STREET GOODS

G.W.R. HIGH STREET PASS.
Com. Yards Patent Fuel Works 263ᵐ81ᶜ
NORTH DOCK GOODS 263ᵐ35ᶜ M.R.
WIND STREET JUNCTION
RUTLAND STREET
VICTORIA STATION

SWANSEA

RIVER TAWE
UPPER BANK
To UPPER BANK
RIVER TANK

WIND ST. G.W. GOODS
L&N.W. GOODS

PRINCE OF WALES DOCK
PORT TENNANT COPPER WORKS
KING'S DOCK

WEST PIER
EAST PIER
ENTRANCE CHANNEL

No. 1 COAL DROPS 264ᵐ25ᶜ
No. 2 COAL DROPS 264ᵐ4ᶜ
Junction (Graving Dock)
MIDLAND COAL HOIST 265ᵐ74ᶜ
Junction of Midland Coal Hoist Sidings 265ᵐ54ᶜ
Future Extension
S.H.T. EMBANKMENT

COAL HOISTS
S.H.T.
To BALDWINS WORKS

MIDLAND RECEPTION & SIDINGS
M.R. KING'S DOCK LINES
Swansea M.R. KING'S DOCK LINES
Junction 265ᵐ24ᶜ
Junction of Sidings 265ᵐ14ᶜ
EAST DOCK JUNCTION 264ᵐ38ᶜ 6.6 SWANSEA MILE
TENNANT CANAL
S.S.A. WAGON WORKS
RHONDDA MID. GREAT

L. AND N.W.R.
SWANSEA AND MUMBLES
30ᶜ

The continuous Distances not in brackets are from St. Pancras Passenger Station by the Shortest Route.
The continuous Distances in brackets are from Swansea St. Thomas' Passenger Station, and represent the Mile Post Mileage (New).

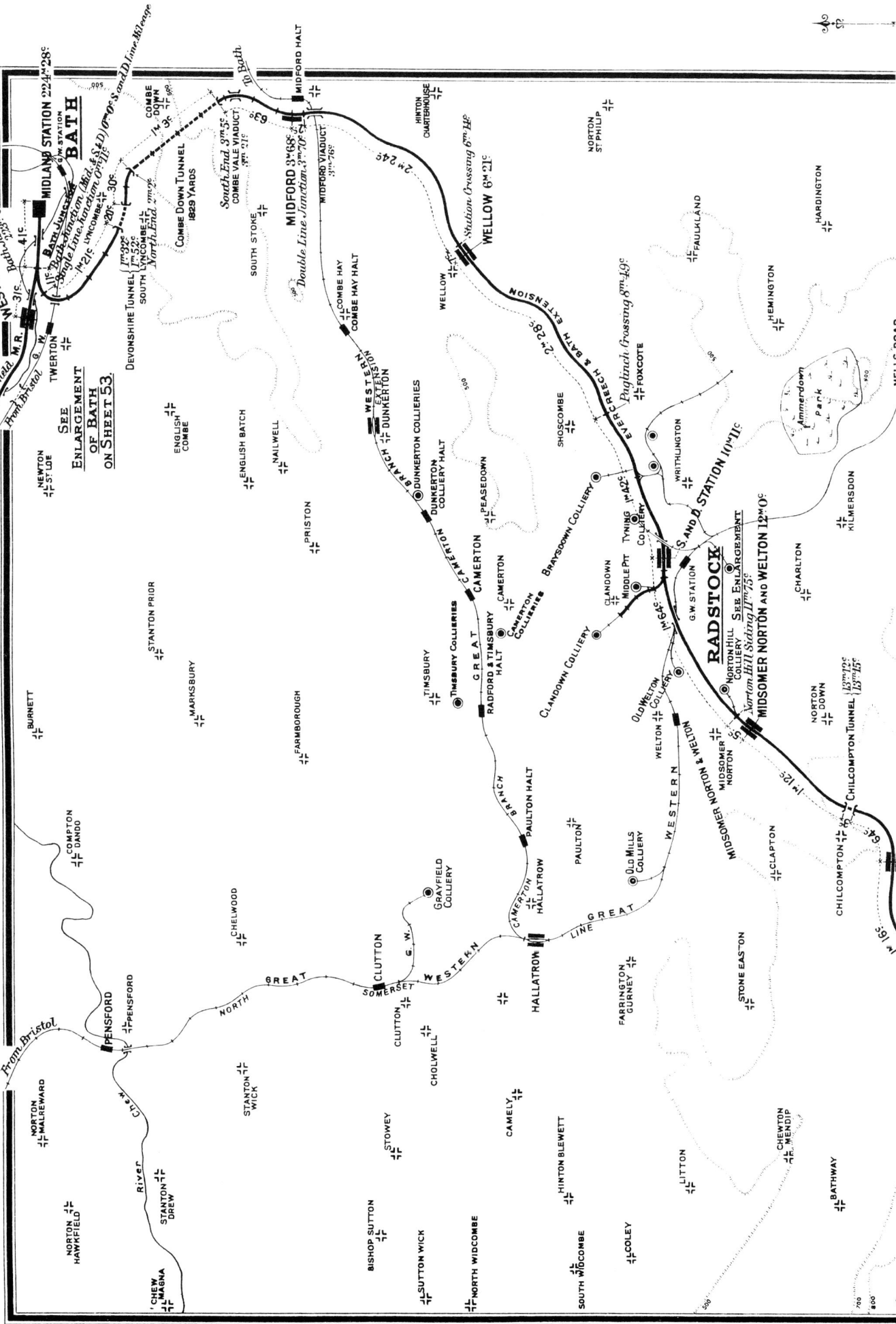

MIDLAND RAILWAY DISTANCE DIAGRAM, SCALE 1 INCH TO 1 MILE.
SOMERSET AND DORSET JOINT LINES.
RADSTOCK DISTRICT.

BOOK Nº 76

SHEET 53.

BATH
MIDLAND STATION 224ᴹ28ᶜ
G.W. STATION

WESTON 223ᴹ86ᶜ
Bath Junction 223ᴹ66ᶜ
Bath Junction (Mid. & S.&D) G.W.'s and S.&D Line Mileage
Single Line Junction 0ᴹ11ᶜ
LYNCOMBE 1ᴹ21ᶜ
41ᶜ
31ᶜ
20ᶜ 30ᶜ

From Mangotsfield M.R.
From Bristol G.W.
TWERTON

NEWTON ST. LOE

SEE
ENLARGEMENT
OF BATH
ON SHEET 53.

Devonshire Tunnel {1ᴹ32ᶜ / 1ᴹ52ᶜ}
SOUTH LYNCOMBE
NORTH END
Combe Down Tunnel 1ᴹ21ᶜ
1829 YARDS

COMBE DOWN

MIDFORD HALT
To Bath

South End 3ᴹ5ᶜ
COMBE VALE VIADUCT
Double Line Junction 3ᴹ70ᶜ
2ᴹ71ᶜ
MIDFORD 3ᴹ68ᶜ
MIDFORD VIADUCT 3ᴹ76ᶜ
63ᶜ

ENGLISH COMBE
ENGLISH BATCH
NAILWELL
SOUTH STOKE

COMBE HAY
COMBE HAY HALT

WESTERN EXTENSION BRANCH
DUNKERTON
DUNKERTON COLLIERIES
DUNKERTON COLLIERY HALT
PEASEDOWN

HINTON CHARTERHOUSE
NORTON ST. PHILIP

WELLOW 6ᴹ21ᶜ
Station Crossing 6ᴹ14ᶜ
WELLOW
2ᴹ24ᶜ
2ᴹ28ᶜ

EVERCREECH & BATH EXTENSION
Paglinch Crossing 8ᴹ49ᶜ
FOXCOTE

FAULKLAND
HEMINGTON
HARDINGTON

Amerdown Park
MELLS ROAD

STANTON PRIOR
MARKSBURY
PRISTON
FARMBOROUGH

SHOSCOMBE
BRAYSDOWN COLLIERY

BURNETT

TIMSBURY COLLIERIES
TIMSBURY
GREAT CAMERTON BRANCH
CAMERTON
CAMERTON COLLIERIES
RADFORD & TIMSBURY HALT

CLANDOWN
MIDDLE PIT
CLANDOWN COLLIERY

TYNING 11ᴹ42ᶜ
Colliery
11ᴹ44ᶜ
S. AND D. STATION 11ᴹ11ᶜ
RADSTOCK
G.W. STATION
SEE ENLARGEMENT

NORTON HILL COLLIERY
Norton Hill Siding 11ᴹ75ᶜ
MIDSOMER NORTON and WELTON 12ᴹ0ᶜ

WRITHLINGTON
KILMERSDON
CHARLTON

COMPTON DANDO

CHELWOOD

GRAYFIELD COLLIERY

PAULTON HALT
CAMERTON BRANCH
HALLATROW
PAULTON
OLD MILLS COLLIERY
WESTERN
OLD WELTON
WELTON COLLIERY

MIDSOMER NORTON
NORTON DOWN
CLAPTON

NORTON MALREWARD

CLUTTON
G.W.
GREAT WESTERN SOMERSET LINE
HALLATROW
CHOLWELL
CAMELY
FARRINGTON GURNEY
STONE EASTON

CHILCOMPTON Tunnel {13ᴹ12ᶜ / 13ᴹ15ᶜ}
CHILCOMPTON
32ᶜ
32½ᴍ
59½

From Bristol
River Chew
PENSFORD
SHEET 53.

NORTON HAWKFIELD
STANTON DREW
CHEW MAGNA

STANTON WICK
STOWEY
BISHOP SUTTON
SUTTON WICK
NORTH WIDCOMBE
SOUTH WIDCOMBE
COLEY
HINTON BLEWETT
CAMELY
LITTON
CHEWTON KEYNSHAM MENDIP
BATHWAY

SHEET 63.

1917.

RADSTOCK

To Frome
To Bath
FOXCOTE COLLIERY
BRAYSDOWN COLLIERY
Braysdown Colliery Sidings 9ᵐ16ᶜ
Writhlington Colliery Sidings 9ᵐ13ᶜ
LOWER WRITHLINGTON COLLIERY
UPPER WRITHLINGTON COLLIERY
TYNING COLLIERY
TRAMWAY
Also THE BRITISH WAGON Cᵒʸ THE RADSTOCK COAL Cᵒʸ AND THE COOPERATIVE SOCIETY'S SIDINGS
LUDLOWS COLLIERY
CLANDOWN TRAMWAY JUNCTION 10ᵐ7ᶜ
S. AND D. STATION 10ᵐ1ᶜ
ENGINE & CARRIAGE 10ᵐ21ᶜ
TRAFFIC 10ᵐ55ᶜ
G. W. STATION
G.W.R. BRIDGE 10ᵐ55ᶜ
HUISH COLLIERY
G. W.
To Frome
CLANDOWN COLLIERY
End of S. & D. 10ᵐ61ᶜ
MIDDLE PIT 10ᵐ61ᶜ
SOMERSET AND DORSET
WALDEGRAVES 10ᵐ21ᶜ
INCLINE
37ᶜ
38ᶜ
G. W.
KILMERSDON COLLIERY
From Bristol
EVERCREECH
38ᶜ

S O M E R S E T

To Frome
DENHAM
GREAT ELM
EGFORD
MELLS
NEWBURY
UPPER VOBSTER
VOBSTER
BABINGTON
GREAT WESTERN RAILWAY
RADSTOCK BRANCH

CHILCOMPTON 13ᵐ79ᶜ also the New Rock Colliery Siding
Moorewood Colliery Sidings 15ᵐ15ᶜ
Old Down Siding 15ᵐ24ᶜ
Downside College
STRATTON ON THE FOSSE
NEW ROCK COLLIERY
(Emborough Stone Gᵒʸ)
Head & Sons Siding Mendip Stone Works 16ᵐ38ᶜ
NETTLEBRIDGE
The Oakhill Brewery Cᵒˢ Siding 16ᵐ50ᶜ also Dalleys Stone Siding
BINEGAR 16ᵐ44ᶜ
GURNEY SLADE
ASHWICK
HOLCOMBE
EGFORD COLLIERY
HIGHBURY
CLOFORD
LEIGH-ON-MENDIP
DOWNHEAD
STOKE LANE
Quarry
Cranmore Tower
Mendip Granite Quarries

M e n d i p   H i l l s
EMBOROUGH
EAST HORRINGTON
Summit of Line 17ᵐ55ᶜ Altitude 811 feet
MASBURY 18ᵐ10ᶜ
BINEGAR
Beauchamps Winsor Hill Quarry Siding 19ᵐ50ᶜ
Hamwood Viaduct 19ᵐ32ᶜ
Hamwood Siding 19ᵐ40ᶜ
WINSOR HILL TUNNELS
Down Line 19ᵐ63ᶜ Up Line 19ᵐ51ᶜ 19ᵐ60ᶜ
WINSOR HILL 19ᵐ40ᶜ
Downside Quarry Siding 19ᵐ74ᶜ
OAKHILL
CHELYNCH
DOULTING Quarries
BODDEN
BOWLISH
CROSCOMBE
DINDER
WEST SHEPTON
WEST COMPTON

CHARLTON VIADUCT 20ᵐ
BATH ROAD VIADUCT 20ᵐ31ᶜ
CHARLTON G.W. BRIDGE 21ᵐ42ᶜ Nᵒ 87
S. AND D. STATION 21ᵐ27ᶜ
G. STATION
SHEPTON MALLET

DOULTING
CRANMORE
WEST CRANMORE
EAST CRANMORE
CHESTERBLADE
HIGHER ALHAM
BATCOMBE
WESTCOMBE
STONEY STRATTON
MILTON CLEVEDON
River Alham
WANSTROW
WESTONTOWN
UPTON NOBLE
WITHAM
BORDER
NORTH BREWHAM
SOUTH BREWHAM

GREAT WESTERN WITHAM BRANCH
WELLS AND WEST SOMERSET LINE
WILTS SOMERSET AND WEYMOUTH LINE
GREAT WESTERN AND WEYMOUTH LINE
From Wells
From Evercreech

FARNCOMBE
EAST COMPTON
PILTON
WORMINSTER
Pennard Hill
EAST PENNARD
LITTLE PENNARD
PYLLE
HAMBRIDGE

Priestleigh Viaduct 22ᵐ78ᶜ
Station Loop 22ᵐ27ᶜ (1ᵐ88ᶜ) PRIESTLEIGH
PYLE 21ᵐ42ᶜ
Station Loop
EVERCREECH (VILLAGE) 24ᵐ31ᶜ
EVERCREECH JUNCTION
Evercreech Junction 25ᵐ49ᶜ
The Somerset Trading Cᵒˢ Tile & Brick Siding 25ᵐ55ᶜ
Engine & Carriage Siding 25ᵐ65ᶜ
Viaduct 25ᵐ81ᶜ
EVERCREECH JUNCTION STATION 25ᵐ73ᶜ
(0ᵐ0ᶜ Burnham Line)
Station Crossing 25ᵐ77ᶜ
Single Line Junction 25ᵐ60ᶜ
Evercreech Junction (0ᵐ0ᶜ Burnham Line) 25ᵐ49ᶜ
DITCHEAT
To Bournemouth

SOMERSET CENTRAL BRANCH
BURNHAM AND EVERCREECH BRANCH
1ᵐ47ᶜ
WEST PENNARD 30ᵐ57ᶜ
37ᶜ
Cockmill Crossing 30ᵐ24ᶜ (4ᵐ51ᶜ)
Steam Bow Crossing 30ᵐ24ᶜ (4ᵐ51ᶜ)
From Burnham

SHEET 61.

The continuous Distances are from BATH JUNCTION and represent the Mile Post Mileage, except on the Burnham Line, where the latter is in brackets.

MENDIP HILLS

S O M E R S E T

GREAT WESTERN

CHEDDAR VALLEY WESTBURY

Cheddar Cliffs

PRIDDY

DRAYCOTT
DRAYCOTT

RODNEY STOKE

LODGE HILL
WESTBURY

CHEDDAR

AXBRIDGE

WEARE

BADGWORTH

STONE ALLERTON

CHAPEL ALLERTON

RIVER YEO

COCKLAKE

WEDMORE

BLACKFORD

MUDGLEY

WESTHAY

RIVER AXE

BAGLEY

HENTON

YARLEY

WOOKEY

WOOKEY

WELLS

G.W. STATION

S. AND D. STATION

West Junction with G.W.R. 41ᴹ·35ᶜ(5ᴹ·39ᶜ)
Junction 41ᴹ·31ᶜ(5ᴹ·35ᶜ)
S. and D. STATION 41ᴹ·34ᶜ(5ᴹ·38ᶜ)
East Junction with G.W.R. 41ᴹ·36ᶜ(5ᴹ·40ᶜ) Ex
Glastonbury

To Witham

G W
WELLS & WITHAM

35ᴹ·25ᶜ

Oxley Crossing 40ᴹ·19ᶜ(4ᴹ·16ᶜ)

SEE ENLARGEMENT

Queen's Sedge Moor

LAUNCHERLEY

NORTH WOOTTON

WEST PENNARD 30ᴹ·75ᶜ(3ᴹ·8ᶜ)
Sub.Loop West 30ᴹ·68ᶜ(5ᴹ·19ᶜ)
Station Level Crossing 30ᴹ·74ᶜ(3ᴹ·8ᶜ)
Sub.Loop East 30ᴹ·76ᶜ(5ᴹ·23ᶜ)

To Evercreech Junction

Brunel Lane Crossing 31ᴹ·58ᶜ(3ᴹ·40ᶜ)

BURNHAM AND EVERCREECH

3ᴹ·20ᶜ

1ᴹ·50ᶜ

COXLEY

POLSHAM 39ᴹ·3ᶜ(3ᴹ·7ᶜ)
Station Level Crossing 39ᴹ·2ᶜ(3ᴹ·6ᶜ)

POLSHAM

WELLS

BRANCH

36ᴹ

STATION SEE ENLARGEMENT

Cemetery Lane Crossing

73ᶜ

Wells branch Junction 38ᴹ·16ᶜ(0ᴹ·18ᶜ)
Cemetery Crossing 38ᴹ·18ᶜ(0ᴹ·25ᶜ)

73ᶜ

GODNEY

Aqueduct Crossing 37ᴹ·45ᶜ(1ᴹ·46ᶜ)

Sharpham Crossing 36ᴹ·35ᶜ(1ᴹ·11ᶜ)

ASHCOTT 38ᴹ·36ᶜ(3ᴹ·75ᶜ)
Station Level Crossing 38ᴹ·35ᶜ(3ᴹ·69ᶜ)

MEARE

RIVER BRUE

Ham Wall Bridge and the Edington Siding

40ᶜ

(SOMERSET CENTRAL)

3ᶜ

EVERCREECH
1ᴹ·65ᶜ

SHAPWICK
Sub.Loop West 40ᴹ·58ᶜ(15ᴹ·29ᶜ)
FOR WESTHAY & MEARE 40ᴹ·50ᶜ(15ᴹ·12ᶜ)
Station Level Crossing 40ᴹ·57ᶜ(15ᴹ·15ᶜ)
Sub.Loop East 40ᴹ·59ᶜ(15ᴹ·31ᶜ)

Catcott Crossing 41ᴹ·38ᶜ(16ᴹ·49ᶜ)

Bason Bridge Canton Swing Bridge (19ᴹ·49ᶜ)

AND

1ᴹ·40ᶜ

4ᶜ

EDINGTON JUNCTION STATION
Sub.Loop West 42ᴹ·27ᶜ(17ᴹ·66ᶜ)
Station Level Crossing 42ᴹ·30ᶜ(17ᴹ·70ᶜ)
FOR WEDMORE & Bridgwater Branch
42ᴹ·21ᶜ(17ᴹ·57ᶜ)
Sub.Loop East 42ᴹ·30ᶜ(17ᴹ·73ᶜ)

Edington Junction ex Evercreech Junction
46ᴹ·23ᶜ(20ᴹ·54ᶜ)

BASON BRIDGE

BURNHAM BRANCH

BRIDGWATER BRANCH

From Highbridge

From Bridgwater

3ᴹ·32ᶜ

2ᴹ·75ᶜ

COSSINGTON 45ᴹ·66ᶜ(2ᴹ·75ᶜ)

EDINGTON

CATCOTT

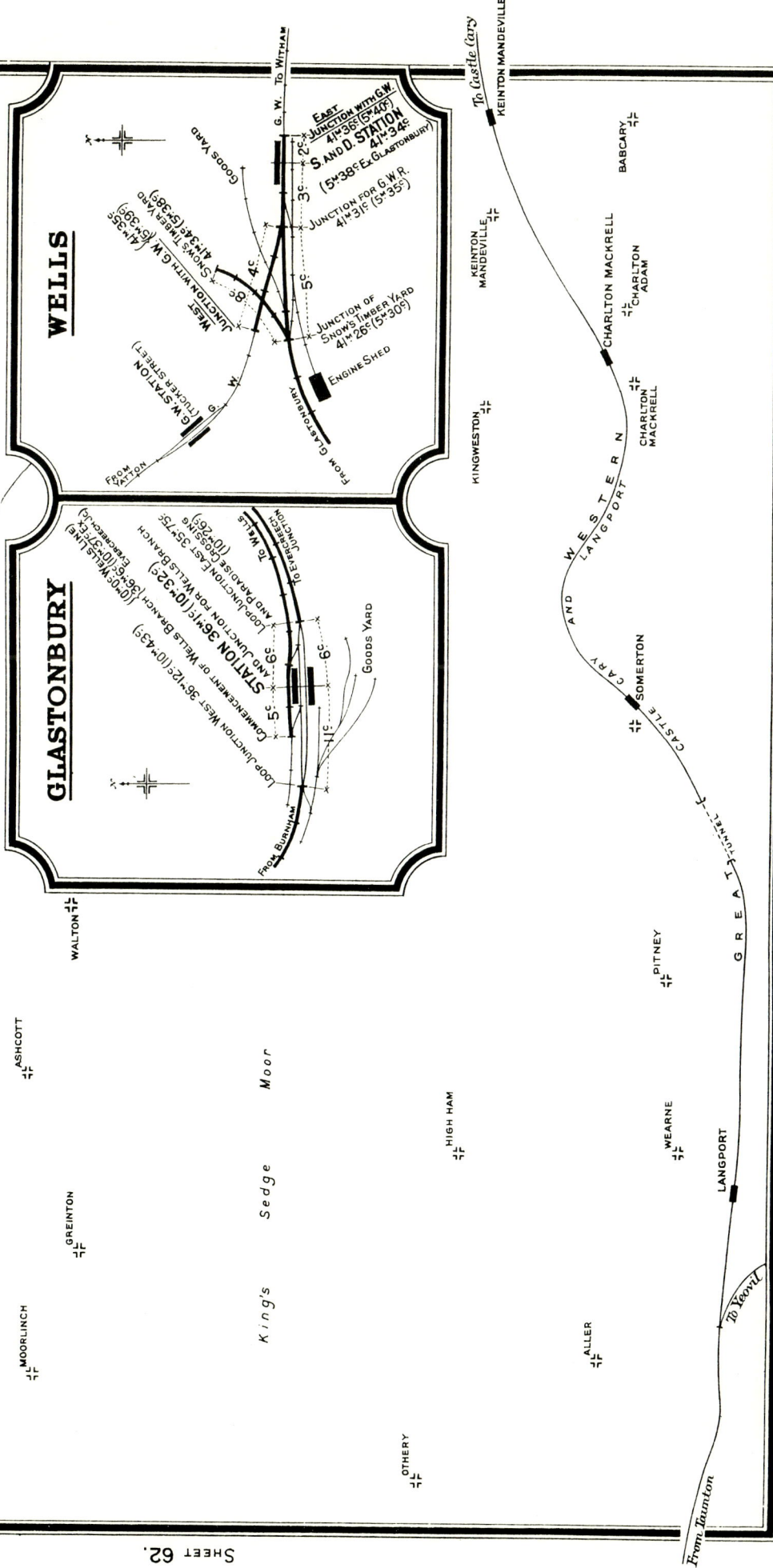

GLASTONBURY
AND STREET

GLASTONBURY

COMMENCEMENT WEST 36ᴹ12ᶜ (10ᴹ43ᶜ)
STATION 36ᴹ1ᶜ (10ᴹ32ᶜ)
2ᴺᴰ JUNCTION FOR WELLS BRANCH (36ᴹ6ᶜ)(10ᴹ37ᶜx)
LOOP JUNCTION EAST 35ᴹ75ᶜ
TO WELLS
TO EVERCREECH JUNCTION
LOOP JUNCTION (EAST WELLS BRANCH)
2ᴺᴰ JUNCTION FOR WELLS BRANCH 35ᴹ75ᶜ
AND PARADISE CROSSING (10ᴹ26ᶜ)
(EVERCREECH Jᴺ)
GOODS YARD
5ᶜ
6ᶜ
11ᶜ
FROM BURNHAM

WELLS

G.W. TO WITHAM
EAST
JUNCTION WITH G.W.
41ᴹ36ᶜ(5ᴹ40ᶜ)
S. AND D. STATION 41ᴹ34ᶜ
(5ᴹ38ᶜ Ex GLASTONBURY)
JUNCTION FOR G.W.R.
41ᴹ31ᶜ (5ᴹ35ᶜ)
JUNCTION OF
SNOW'S TIMBER YARD
41ᴹ26ᶜ (5ᴹ30ᶜ)
ENGINE SHED
GOODS YARD
WEST
JUNCTION WITH G.W. (5ᴹ39ᶜ)
SNOW'S TIMBER YARD 41ᴹ34ᶜ
41ᴹ35ᶜ
L.W. STATION
(TUCKER STREET)
FROM WATTON
FROM GLASTONBURY
3ᶜ
2ᶜ
3ᶜ
5ᶜ
4ᶜ
8ᶜ
W

To Castle Cary
KEINTON MANDEVILLE
KEINTON MANDEVILLE
BABCARY
CHARLTON MACKRELL
CHARLTON ADAM
CHARLTON MACKRELL
CHARLTON MACKRELL
KINGSWESTON
AND WESTERN
LANGPORT
CARY
CASTLE
SOMERTON
PITNEY
WEARNE
LANGPORT
HIGH HAM
ALLER
OTHERY
GREAT TUNNEL
To Yeovil
From Taunton

WEST PENNARD
WALTON
ASHCOTT
SHAPWICK
MOORLINCH
GREINTON
King's Sedge Moor

Sheet 62.

The continuous Distances not in brackets are from BATH JUNCTION.
The continuous Distances in brackets represent the Mile Post Mileage.

BOOK Nº 76

MIDLAND RAILWAY DISTANCE DIAGRAM. SCALE 1 INCH TO 1 MILE.
SOMERSET AND DORSET JOINT LINES.
GLASTONBURY DISTRICT.

1919.

SHEET 61.
(Fourth Edition.)

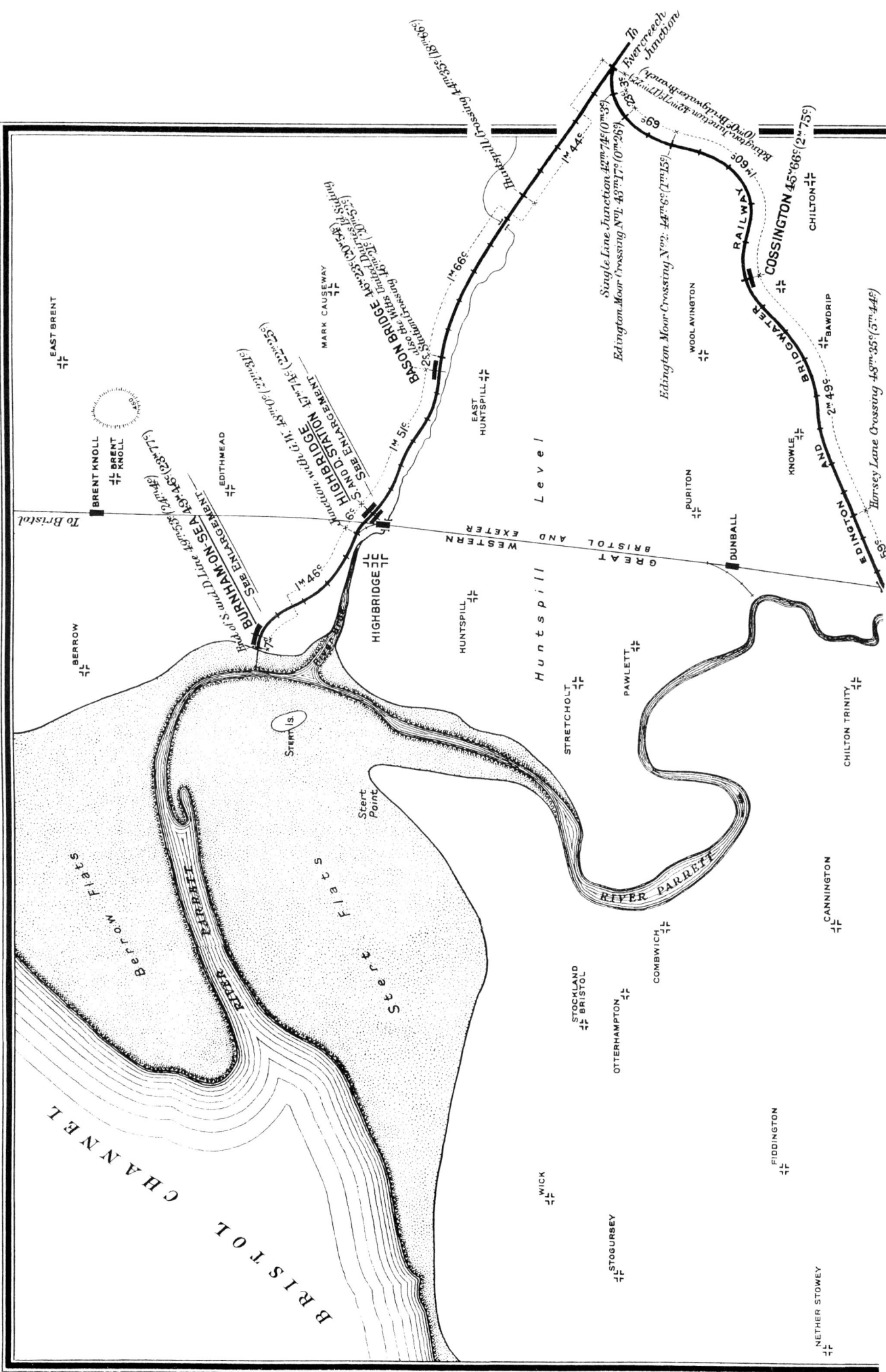

MIDLAND RAILWAY DISTANCE DIAGRAM. SCALE 1 INCH TO 1 MILE.
SOMERSET AND DORSET JOINT LINES.
HIGHBRIDGE DISTRICT.

BOOK No 76

BRISTOL CHANNEL

Berrow Flats

RIVER PARRETT

Stert Is.

Stert Flats

Stert Point

Huntspill Level

RIVER PARRETT

BERROW

BRENT KNOLL
BRENT KNOLL

EAST BRENT

EDITHMEAD

To Bristol

To Bristol

BURNHAM-ON-SEA
SEE ENLARGEMENT

HIGHBRIDGE
HIGHBRIDGE STATION 17ᵐ 74ᶜ
S AND D. SEE ENLARGEMENT

BASON BRIDGE 16ᵐ 23ᶜ(20ᵐ 05ᶜ) Siding
(16ᵐ 05ᶜ) Loop (17ᵐ 15ᶜ) Siding
Junction with G.W.R. 16ᵐ 49ᶜ(17ᵐ 41ᶜ)
Bason the Witts Gate 16ᵐ 11ᶜ
(16ᵐ 05ᶜ) Strum Crossing 16ᵐ 21ᶜ

MARK CAUSEWAY

Bed of S. and D. Line 16ᵐ 55ᶜ(24ᵐ 46ᶜ)(23ᵐ 77ᶜ)

HUNTSPILL
EAST HUNTSPILL

GREAT   WESTERN   AND   BRISTOL   EXETER

DUNBALL

PURITON

KNOWLE

WOOLAVINGTON

STRETCHOLT

PAWLETT

COMBWICH

STOCKLAND BRISTOL

OTTERHAMPTON

CANNINGTON

CHILTON TRINITY

FIDDINGTON

WICK

STOGURSEY

NETHER STOWEY

BAWDRIP

CHILTON

To Evercreech Junction

Huntspill Crossing 14ᵐ 35ᶜ(18ᵐ 49ᶜ)

Single Line Junction 42ᵐ 74ᶜ(0ᵐ 8ᶜ)
Edington Moor Crossing No1. 43ᵐ 17ᶜ(0ᵐ 26ᶜ)
Edington Moor Crossing No2. 44ᵐ 6ᶜ(1ᵐ 15ᶜ)
Edington Junction 42ᵐ 17ᶜ (0ᵐ 0⁵⁹)(Bridgwater Branch)

COSSINGTON 45ᵐ 66ᶜ(2ᵐ 75ᶜ)

EDINGTON AND BRIDGWATER RAILWAY

Horsey Lane Crossing 48ᵐ 35ᶜ(5ᵐ 44ᶜ)

1ᵐ 66ᶜ
1ᵐ 44ᶜ
1ᵐ 66ᶜ
1ᵐ 5ᶜ
1ᵐ 46ᶜ
56ᶜ
56ᶜ
59ᶜ
50ᶜ
2ᵐ 49ᶜ
25ᶜ
35ᶜ

SHEET 61.

1919.

To Yeovil and Reading

STAWELL

SUTTON MALLETT

MIDDLEZOY

WESTON ZOYLAND

S O M E R S E T

STATHE

WESTERN

DURSTON AND YEOVIL

LYNG

GREAT

STOKE ST. GREGORY

WEST LYNG

G.

RIVER TONE

NORTH CURREY

West

Sedge Moor

RIVER PARRETT

ATHELNEY

Cogload Junction

Durston Water Troughs

DURSTON

BRIDGWATER

AND

GREAT WESTERN AND BRISTOL AND EXETER

CANAL

HUNTWORTH HAYES

NORTH PETHERTON

TAUNTON (G.W.R. COY.)

NORTH NEWTON

DURSTON

THURLOXTON

DURLEIGH

G.W.Bridge 49m 14c (6m 23c)
Castle Fields Crossing 49m 62c (6m 71c)
Station Loop 49m 64c (6m 73c)
Wharf Branch Junction 49m 67c (6m 76c) CHEDZOY
S.and D. STATION (49m 79c Ex Bath Junction)
(7m 8c Ex Edington Junction)
G.W. STATION

RIVER WHARF 50m 85c
(7m 44c)
Brickyard Siding 50m 14c (7m 29c)
Station 50m 90c (7m 49c)
Junction 50m

BRIDGWATER

Creech Junction

BATHPOOL

G. W. THORNFALCON
To Chard

WESTERN

RUSHTON

HIGHBRIDGE AND BURNHAM

To Bristol

GREAT WESTERN AND EXETER

BURNHAM-ON-SEA

JETTY

STATION 49m 46c (23m 77c)
(49m 53c Ex Bath Junction)
(24m 4c Ex Evercreech Junc)
End of S. and D. Line
Station Crossing 49m 48c (23m 79c)

50c
60c
29c
9c
9c
9c

HIGHBRIDGE WHARF 48m 50c (23m 1c)
Bland's Timber Yard Siding 48m 29c (22m 60c)
CATTLE DOCKS & Junction 48m 21c (22m 52c)
GOODS SHED 48m 2c (22m 43c)

HIGHBRIDGE

G.W. STATION

Junction of Colthurst Symons & Co. LTD. AND
The Apex Tile & Brick Coy's Brickworks 48m 66c (23m 17c)
Church Street Crossing 48m 12c (22m 43c)
GOODS SHED 48m 3c (22m 34c)
Wharf Branch Junction & Level Crossing 48m 3c (22m 34c)
G.W. Junction 48m 0c (22m 31c)
G.W.R. Level Crossing 47m 79c (22m 30c)
Loop Junction West 47m 77c (22m 28c)
S. and D. STATION 47m 74c (22m 25c)
Highbridge Loop East 47m 71c (22m 22c)
Carriage Works Junction 47m 71c (22m 22c)
Engine Works Junction 47m 63c (22m 14c)
Highbridge Loop East 47m 59c (22m 10c)

To EVERCREECH JUNCTION

FROM EXETER

GREAT WESTERN

Vale of Taunton-Deane

WESTON MONKTON

NORTON FITZWARREN

BISHOP'S HULL

TAUNTON

STATION

NORTON FITZWARREN

G.W. From Minehead
G.W. From Barnstaple
From Exeter

The continuous Distances not in brackets are from BATH JUNCTION.

The continuous Distances in brackets represent the Mile Post Mileage.

MIDLAND RAILWAY DISTANCE DIAGRAM. SCALE 1 INCH TO 1 MILE.
SOMERSET AND DORSET JOINT LINES.
TEMPLECOMBE DISTRICT.

SHEET 60.

SOUTH BREWHAM

BRUTON

Lamyatt Crossing 26ᵐ.67ᶜ
Bruton Road Crossing 27ᵐ.16ᶜ

G.W.Bridge 28ᵐ.35ᶜ
River Brue Viaduct 28ᵐ.43ᶜ
COLE (FOR BRUTON) 28ᵐ.55ᶜ
Pitcombe Viaduct 29ᵐ.0ᶜ

To Frome

PITCOMBE

STONEY STOKE

SHEPTON MONTAGUE

CHARLTON MUSGROVE

BRATTON SEYMOUR

WINCANTON

WINCANTON 32ᵐ.76ᶜ

CUCKLINGTON

STOKE TRISTER

BUCKHORN WESTON

To London (Waterloo)

RIVER CALE

BLACK

1ᵐ 79ᶜ

Cheriton Crossing 34ᵐ.75ᶜ

Goods Yard Junction 35ᵐ.57ᶜ
Templecombe Junction 36ᵐ.43ᶜ

62ᶜ
36ᶜ
34ᶜ

59ᶜ

LOWER GOODS STATION 36ᵐ.36ᶜ

TEMPLECOMBE
— SEE ENLARGEMENT —
JOINT STATION 36ᵐ.47ᶜ
ABBAS COMBE

TEMPLE COMBE

NORTH CHERITON
SOUTH CHERITON
HORSINGTON

HOLTON

MAPERTON

BLACKFORD

COMPTON PAUNCEFOOT

CHARLTON HILL

CHARLTON HORETHORNE

STOWELL

EVERCREECH JUNCTION STATION 25ᵐ.73ᶜ

DITCHEAT
ALHAMPTON
AUNHAM

RIVER BRUE

CASTLE CARY

From Highbridge and Bath
From Twuton
CASTLE CARY & LANGPORT

7ᵏ⁴ᶜ
29ᶜ
20ᶜ
1ᵐ 19ᶜ

WESTERN

GREAT

ANSFORD

CASTLE CARY

GATHAMPTON

VARLINGTON

DORSET CENTRAL
4ᵐ 2¹⁄₂ᶜ

S O M E R S E T

ALFORD

ALFORD HALT

NORTH BARROW

SOUTH BARROW

WESTERN WEYMOUTH LINE

AND

GREAT SOMERSET

NORTH CADBURY

SOUTH CADBURY

SUTTON MONTIS

WESTON BAMPFYLDE

SPARKFORD

QUEEN CAMEL

WEST CAMEL

MARSTON MAGNA

MARSTON MAGNA

CORTON DENHAM

WILTS

CHILTON CANTELO

HORNBLOTTON

EAST LYDFORD

WHEATHILL

1919.

To Bournemouth

STURMINSTER NEWTON 43ᴹ63ᶜ

Common Lane Crossing 37ᵐ13ᶜ
Park Lane Crossing 37ᵐ51ᶜ
HENSTRIDGE 38ᵐ27ᶜ
Plott Lane Crossing 38ᵐ29ᶜ
Marsh Lane Crossing 38ᵐ44ᶜ
South Mead Crossing 38ᵐ61ᶜ
County Boundary 38ᵐ77ᶜ
Drews Lane Crossing 39ᵐ45ᶜ
Station Loop 39ᵐ55ᶜ
STALBRIDGE 39ᵐ65ᶜ
Station Loop & Crossing 39ᵐ69ᶜ

BLACKMORE VALE

3ᵐ74ᶜ
10ᶜ45ᶜ
64ᶜ
56ᶜ
2ᶜ15ᶜ17ᶜ
38ᶜ

SOMERSET
DORSET

Stalbridge Park

STALBRIDGE

HENSTRIDGE
YENSTON

LYDLINCH

STOURTON
CAUNDLE

RIVER LYDDEN

BISHOP
CAUNDLE

HASELBURY
BRYAN

PURSE
CAUNDLE

MILBORNE PORT

WESTERN MAIN LINE

MILBORNE
WICK

COUNTY OF COUNTY
OF

MILBORNE
PORT

GOATHILL

CAUNDLE
MARSH

POYINGTON

OBERNE

YEOVIL AND SOUTH JUNCTION

Sherborne Park

SANDFORD
ORCAS

HOLWAY
HILL

SHERBORNE

SHERBORNE

D   O   R   S   E   T

RIMPTON

NORTON
WOOTTON

LONDON AND SALISBURY

NETHER COMPTON

TRENT

BRADFORD ABBAS

TEMPLECOMBE

Horsington Crossing 35ᴹ56ᶜ
Goods Yard Junction 35ᵐ57ᶜ
(Nº3 Junction)
Gas Works
S.& D. GOODS STATION 36ᵐ36ᶜ
S.& D. PASSENGER STN 36ᵐ38ᶜ
To London
L.and S.W.R.Bridge
L.and S.W. 36ᵐ39ᶜ
To Bournemouth

FROM
BATH
GOODS STATION BRANCH
59ᶜ
T. JUNCTION RY.
TEMPLECOMBE JUNCTION RY.
36ᶜ
30ᶜ

Templecombe Junction 36ᵐ13ᶜ
(Nº2 Junction)

End of S.& D. Maintenance 36ᵐ47ᶜ
(Nº2 Junction)
PASSENGER STATION 36ᵐ47ᶜ
(L.&S.W. AND S.&D. JOINT)
(UPPER STATION)
and Junction with the L.&S.W.

L.& S.W. GOODS STATION

EXCHANGE SIDINGS

FROM EXETER

LEIGH

YETMINSTER
GREAT WESTERN
SOMERSET AND WEYMOUTH
To Weymouth

CHETNOLE

RYME
INTRINSECA

MELBURY
OSMOND

WILTS. SOMERSET
JUNCTION STATION (L.S.W.)

YEOVIL
PEN MILL
L.G.W.
L.S.W.
TOWN STATION
JOINT

COUNTY OF SOMERSET
COUNTY OF DORSET

From Durston
From Exeter

G.W.GOODS

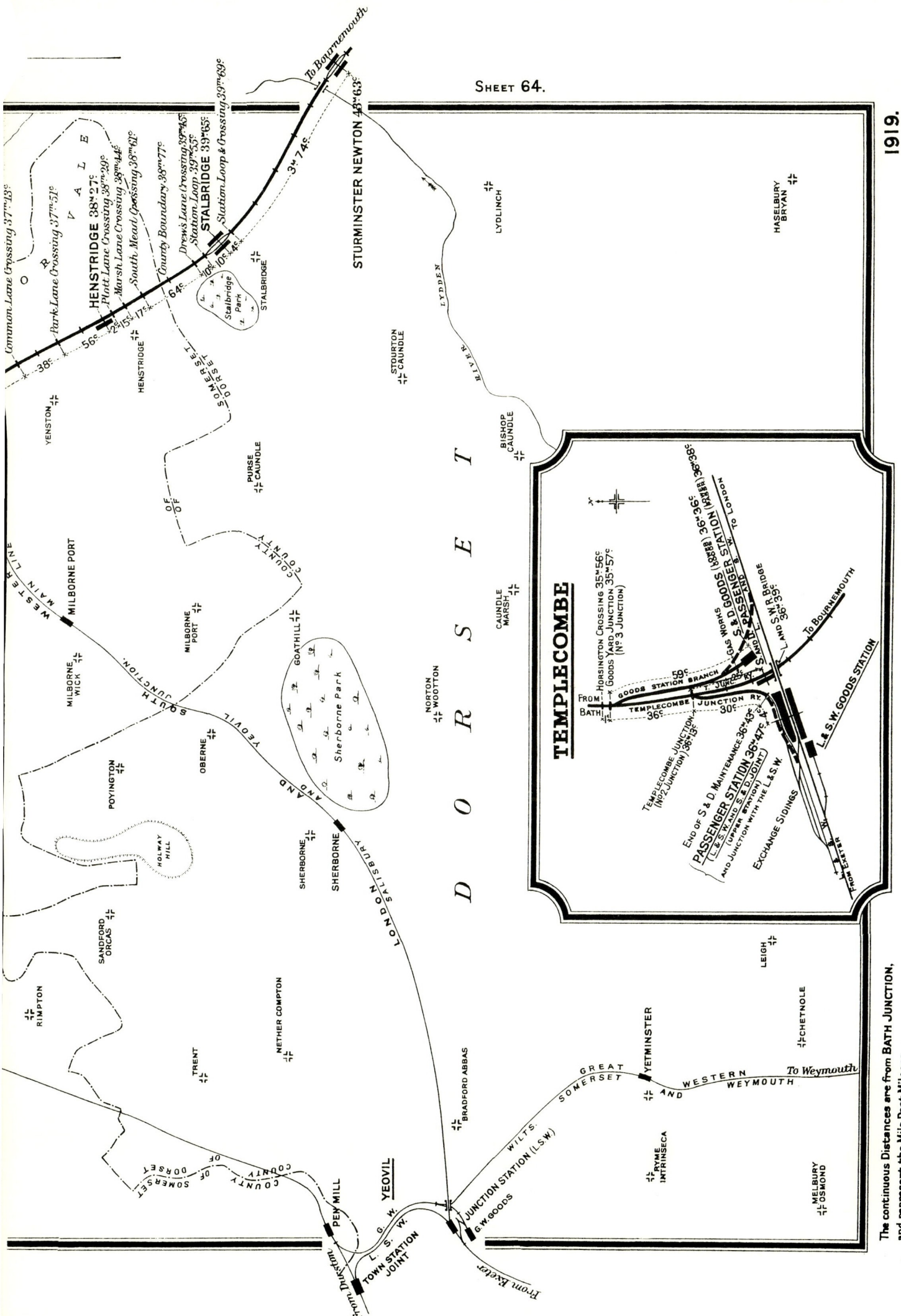

The continuous Distances are from BATH JUNCTION,
and represent the Mile Post Mileage.

MIDLAND RAILWAY DISTANCE DIAGRAM. SCALE 1 INCH TO 1 MILE.
SOMERSET AND DORSET JOINT LINES.
BLANDFORD DISTRICT.

BOOK Nº 76

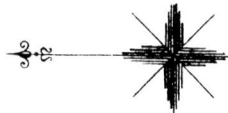

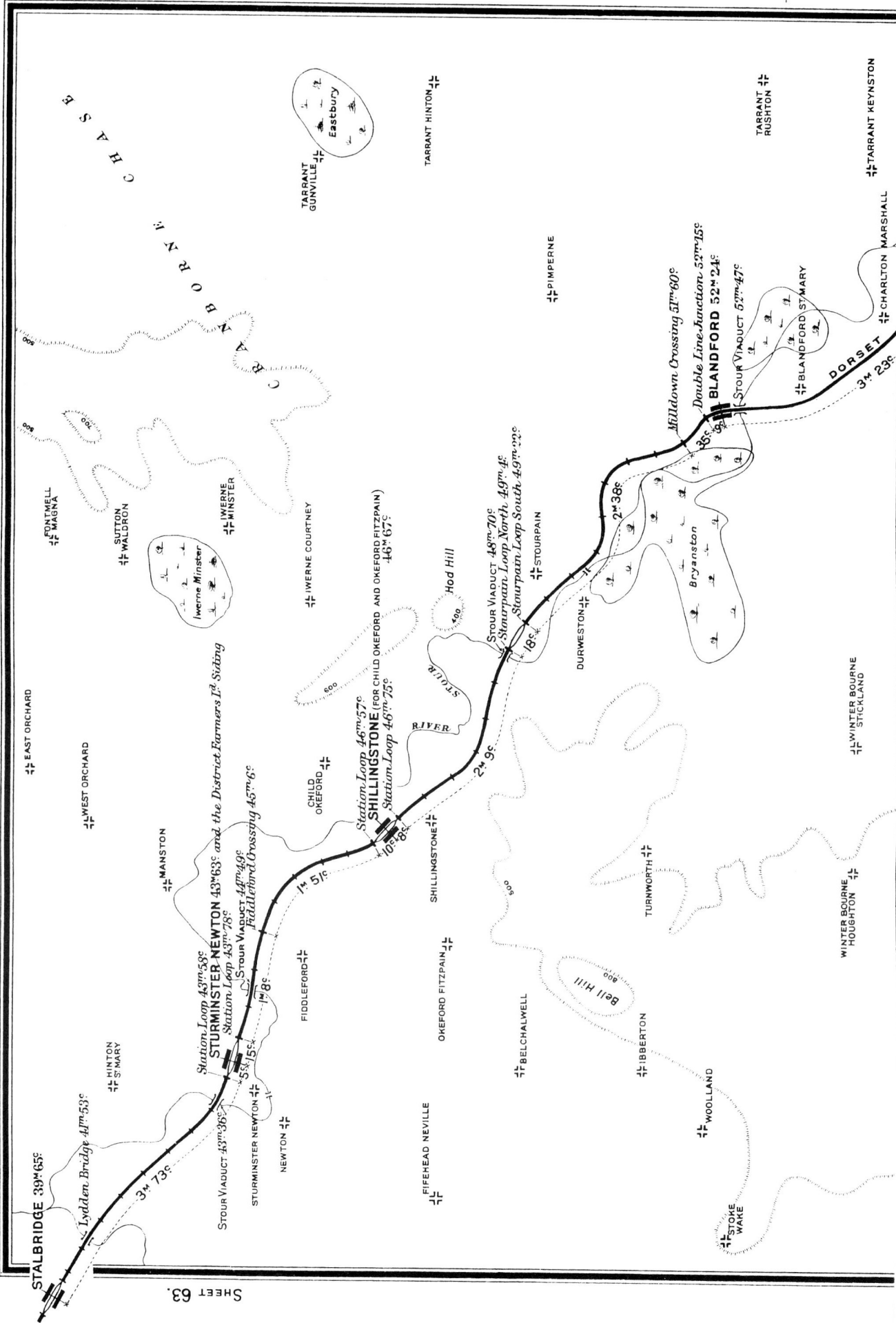

CRANBORNE CHASE

EAST ORCHARD

WEST ORCHARD

FONTMELL MAGNA

SUTTON WALDRON

IWERNE MINSTER

IWERNE MINSTER

IWERNE COURTNEY

TARRANT GUNVILLE

Eastbury

TARRANT HINTON

TARRANT RUSHTON

TARRANT KEYNSTON

CHARLTON MARSHALL

BLANDFORD ST. MARY

PIMPERNE

Stour Viaduct 52ᴹ 47ᶜ

Double Line Junction 52ᴹ 24ᶜ

BLANDFORD 52ᴹ 24ᶜ

Milldown Crossing 51ᴹ 60ᶜ

3ᴹ 23ᶜ

DORSET

36ᶜ 99ᶜ

2ᴹ 38ᶜ

Bryanston

WINTER BOURNE STICKLAND

STOURPAIN

Stourpain Loop South 49ᴹ 22ᶜ

Stourpain Loop North 49ᴹ 4ᶜ

Stour Viaduct 48ᴹ 70ᶜ

DURWESTON

18ᶜ

2ᴹ 9ᶜ

Hod Hill

RIVER STOUR

400

600

600

500

800

TURNWORTH

WINTER BOURNE HOUGHTON

BELL HILL

IBBERTON

BELCHALWELL

WOOLLAND

STOKE WAKE

OKEFORD FITZPAIN

FIFEHEAD NEVILLE

Station Loop 46ᴹ 57ᶜ
SHILLINGSTONE (FOR CHILD OKEFORD AND OKEFORD FITZPAIN)
Station Loop 46ᴹ 75ᶜ

46ᴹ 67ᶜ

10ᶜ 8ᶜ

CHILD OKEFORD

SHILLINGSTONE

FIDDLEFORD

1ᴹ 5ᶜ

Fiddleford Crossing 45ᴹ 6ᶜ

Stour Viaduct 44ᴹ 49ᶜ
Station Loop 43ᴹ 78ᶜ
STURMINSTER NEWTON 43ᴹ 63ᶜ and the District Farmers Lᵈ Siding
Station Loop 43ᴹ 58ᶜ

1ᴹ 8ᶜ

55ᶜ 15ᶜ

Sturminster Newton 43ᴹ 36ᶜ
Stour Viaduct 43ᴹ 36ᶜ

NEWTON

MANSTON

HINTON ST. MARY

3ᴹ 73ᶜ

Lydden Bridge 41ᴹ 53ᶜ

STALBRIDGE 39ᴹ 65ᶜ

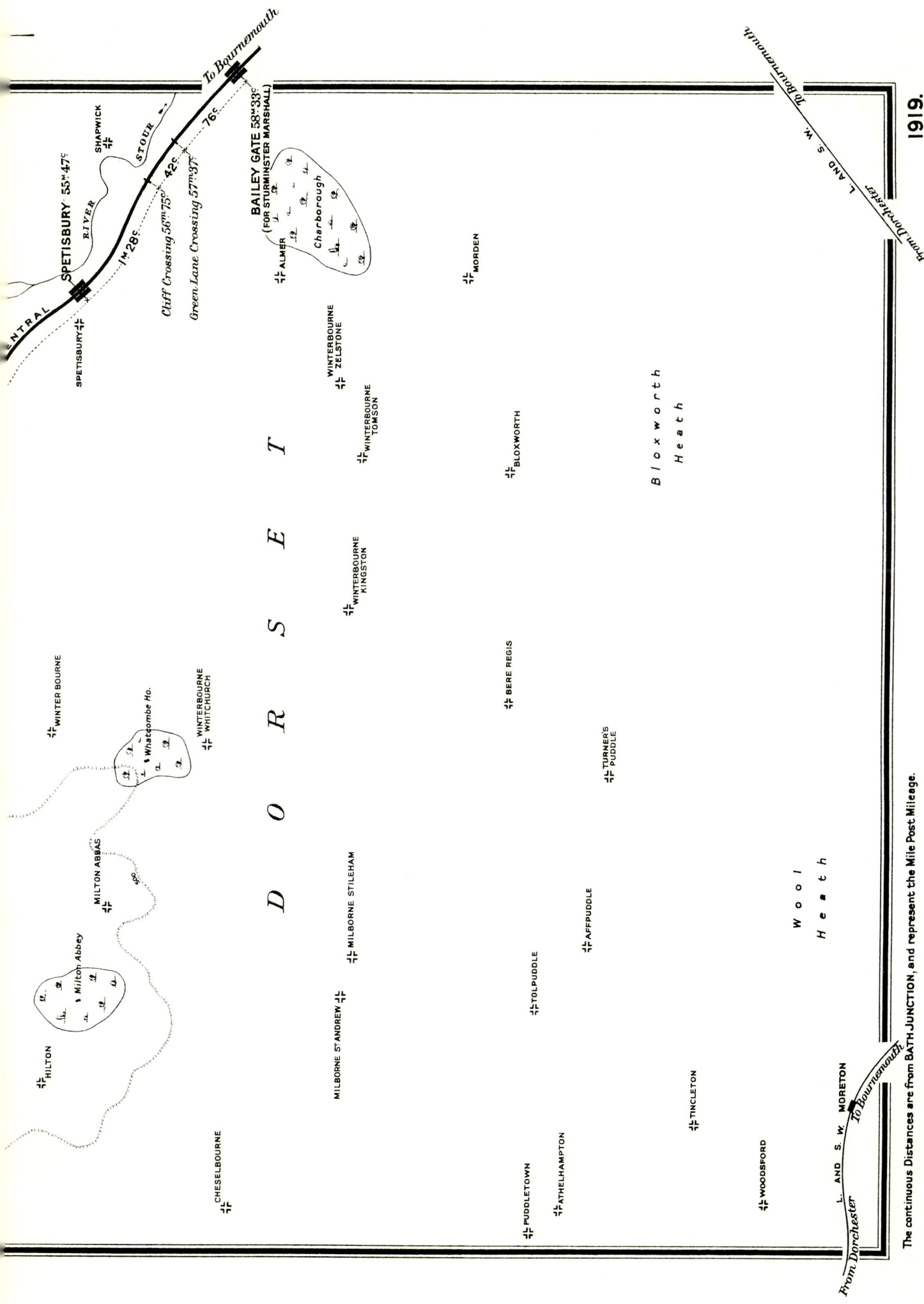

1919.

L. AND S. W.

From Dorchester

To Bournemouth

To Bournemouth

SPETISBURY. 55ᵐ·47ᶜ

SHAPWICK

STOUR RIVER

NTRAL

76ᶜ

42ᶜ

1ᵐ·28ᶜ

Cliff Crossing 56ᵐ·75ᶜ

Green Lane Crossing 57ᵐ·37ᶜ

SPETISBURY

BAILEY GATE 58ᵐ·33ᶜ
(FOR STURMINSTER MARSHALL)

ALMER

Charborough

MORDEN

WINTERBOURNE ZELSTONE

WINTERBOURNE TOMSON

BLOXWORTH

Bloxworth Heath

WINTERBOURNE KINGSTON

BERE REGIS

TURNER'S PUDDLE

WINTER BOURNE

Whatcombe Ho.

WINTERBOURNE WHITCHURCH

D O R S E T

MILTON ABBAS

Milton Abbey

HILTON

MILBORNE ST ANDREW

MILBORNE STILEHAM

800

TOLPUDDLE

AFFPUDDLE

Wool Heath

CHESELBOURNE

PUDDLETOWN

ATHELHAMPTON

TINCLETON

WOODSFORD

MORETON

To Bournemouth

From Dorchester

To Bournemouth

From Dorchester

The continuous Distances are from BATH JUNCTION, and represent the Mile Post Mileage.

MIDLAND RAILWAY DISTANCE DIAGRAM. SCALE 1 INCH TO 1 MILE.
SOMERSET AND DORSET JOINT LINES.
BOURNEMOUTH DISTRICT.

BOOK No 76

To Southampton

To Southampton

L. & S. W.
From Salisbury

WEST MOORS

WEST HURN

HOLDENHURST

POKESDOWN

W. LINE
BOURNEMOUTH DIRECT
(CHRISTCHURCH AND B'MOUTH)

AND BOSCOMBE
BOSCOMBE

CENTRAL (PASSENGER STATION)

CENTRAL (GOODS)
(RINGWOOD)

L. AND S. W.

BOURNEMOUTH
WEST STATION 70 M 77 C

PIER

PIER

H A N T S

WEST PARLEY

WINTON

METRICK PARK HALT

Junction 70 M 12 C

69 M 39 C
69 M 63 C

BRANKSOME 69 M 39 C

29 C
65 C

BRANKSOME

KINSON

RIVER STOUR

HAMPRESTON

Canford Park

DORSET
HANTS
OF
OF
COUNTY
COUNTY

PARKSTONE 68 M 84 C
45 C
1 M 25 C
AND S. W.

POOLE AND BOURNEMOUTH

D O R S E T

Holes Bay Junction 66 M 72 C

POOLE 66 M 50 C

45 C

HAMWORTHY
JUNCTION

L. AND S. W.

L. AND S. W.

QUAY

2 M 73 C

HINTON PARVA

WIMBORNE **63 M 44 C**

Wimborne Junction 63 M 49 C
(S. & D. with L. & S. W.)

WIMBORNE
MINSTER

18 C

1 M 30 C

1 M 33 C

Lake Heath

DORSET CENTRAL

CORFE MULLEN

JUNCTION LINE 62 C

1 M 79 C

Broadstone Junction (S. & D. with L. & S. W.) 63 M 6 C

Broadstone Junction
BROADSTONE 63 M 12 C

6 C

Loop Junction 63 M 0 C

Kingston
Lacy

Bailey Gate Crossing 59 M 63 C
(Corfe Mullen)

Admiralty Siding 59 M 72 C

Lake Crossing 61 M 14 C

Carter's Siding 60 M 42 C

Darbies's Siding 60 M 18 C

CORFE MULLEN
JUNCTION

48 C

26 C

STURMINSTER MARSHALL
(and Corfe & Dorset)

BAILEY GATE 58 M 33 C

Modern, Darbies La Siding

1 M 30 C

From Bath

LYTCHETT
MINSTER

LYTCHETT
MATRAVERS

L. AND S. W.

SOUTHAMPTON

L. AND DORCHESTER

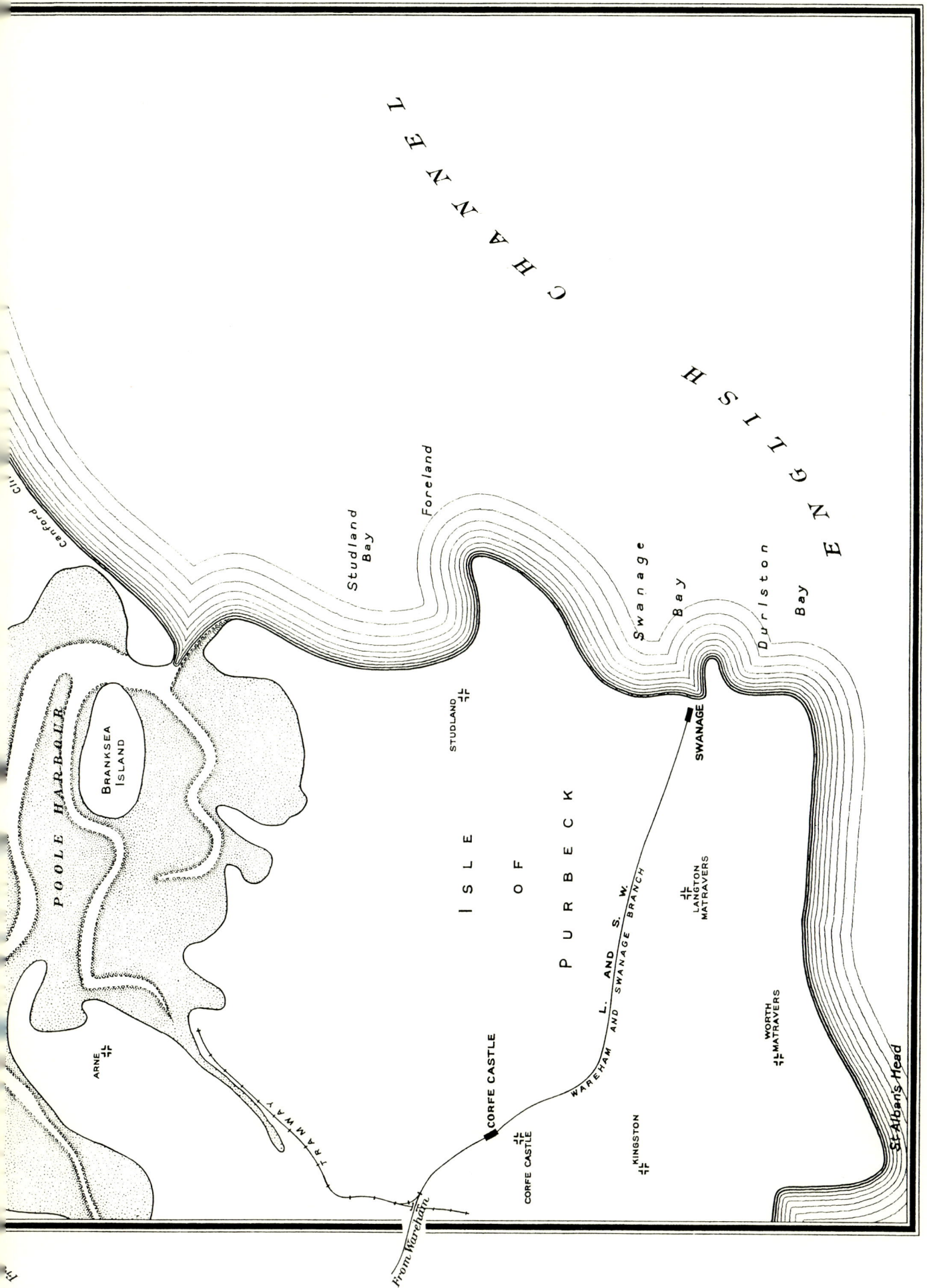

CHANNEL

ENGLISH

Canford Cliffs

POOLE HARBOUR

BRANKSEA
ISLAND

Studland
Bay

Foreland

Swanage
Bay

Durlston
Bay

STUDLAND

SWANAGE

ARNE

ISLE
OF
PURBECK

TRAMWAY

LANGTON
MATRAVERS

From Wareham

CORFE CASTLE

CORFE CASTLE

KINGSTON

WORTH
MATRAVERS

WAREHAM AND SWANAGE BRANCH
L. AND S. W.

St. Alban's Head

The continuous Distances are from BATH JUNCTION, and on the S.&D. Lines represent the Mile Post Mileage.

1919.

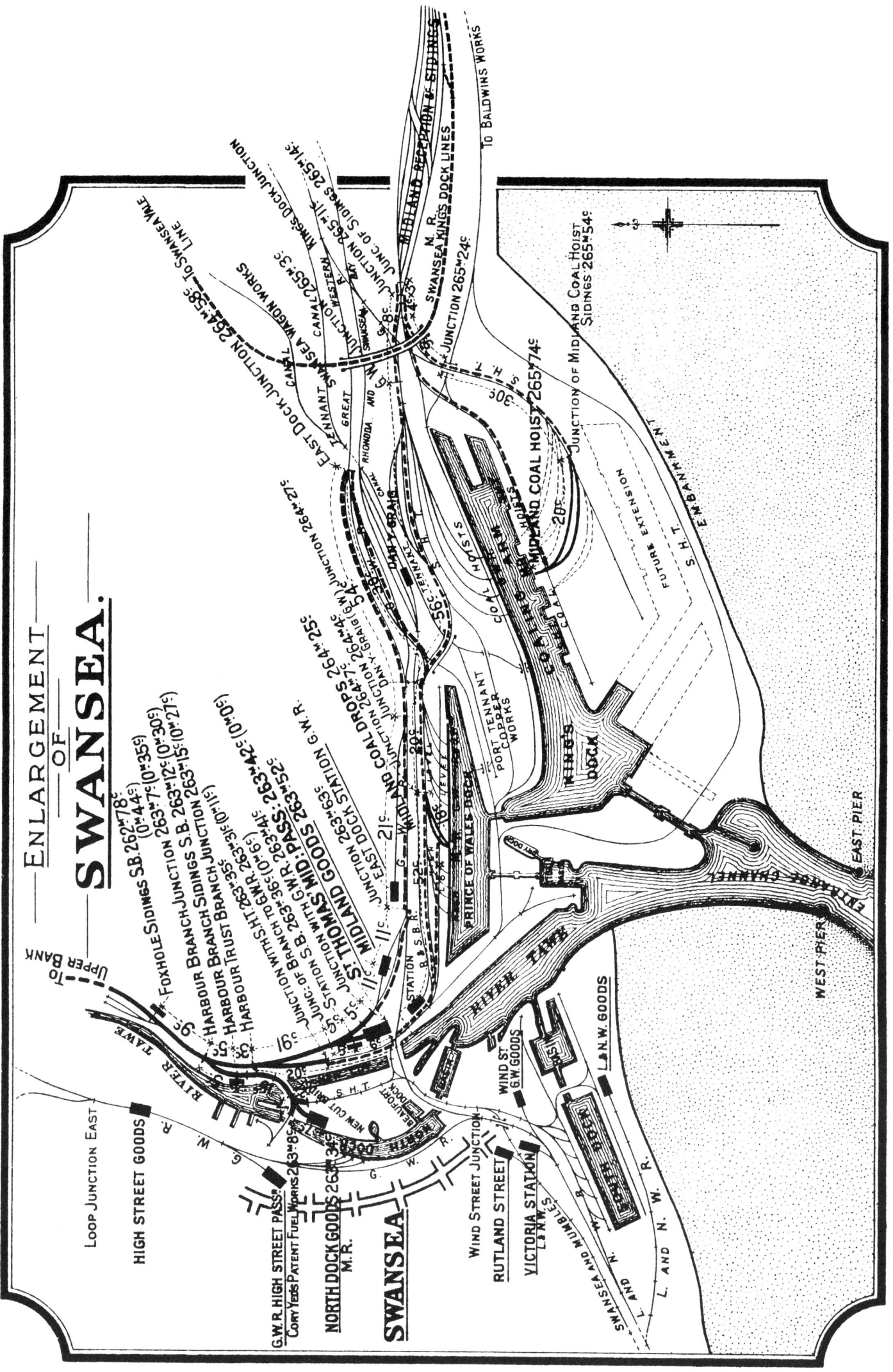

ENLARGEMENT
— OF —
SWANSEA.

Foxhole Sidings S.B. 262m78c
(0m44c)
Harbour Branch Junction 263m7c (0m35c)
Harbour Branch Sidings S.B. 263m12c (0m30c)
Harbour Branch Junction 263m15c (0m27c)
Harbour Trust Branch Junction 263m35c (0m11c)
Junction with S.H.T. 263m35½c (0m6c)
Junction of Branch 263m36c (0m4c)
Junc: of S.B. 263m41c
Junc:n S.B. with G.W.R. 263m42c (0m0c)
Station S.B. with G.W.R. PASS: 263m52c
ST. THOMAS' MID: PASS: 263m63c
St. MIDLAND GOODS Station G.W.R.

Junction 264m27c
Junction 264m25c
East Dock Coal Drops 264m7c 264m4c (G.W.)
Midland Coal Drops 264m7c
Junction with Dan-Y-Graig

SWANSEA

LOOP JUNCTION EAST

HIGH STREET GOODS

G.W.R. HIGH STREET PASS.
Cory Yards Patent Fuel Works 263m85c
NORTH DOCK GOODS 26m34m55c
M.R.

WIND ST.
G.W. GOODS

RUTLAND STREET

VICTORIA STATION
L. & N.W.S.

SWANSEA AND MUMBLES

To UPPER BANK

RIVER TAWE

BEAUFORT DOCK

NEW CUT BRIDGE

NORTH DOCK

WIND STREET JUNCTION

FLOATING DOCK

PRINCE OF WALES DOCK

RIVER TAWE

WEST PIER

EAST PIER

ENTRANCE CHANNEL

KING'S DOCK

PORT TENNANT COPPER WORKS

COAL HOISTS

COALING ARM

MIDLAND COAL HOIST 265m74c

FUTURE EXTENSION

S.H.T. EMBANKMENT

JUNCTION OF MIDLAND COAL HOIST SIDINGS 265m54c

SWANSEA KING'S DOCK LINES

MIDLAND RECEPTION & SIDINGS

To BALDWINS WORKS

DAN-Y-GRAIG

EAST DOCK JUNCTION 264m38c

To SWANSEA VALE LINE

SWANSEA DOCK JUNCTION

KING'S DOCK SIDINGS 265m11c

JUNC:N OF SIDINGS 265m41c

JUNCTION 265m24c

JUNCTION 265m30c